DATE D

The Limits of Law-Based School Reform

The Limits of Law-Based School Reform

VAIN HOPES AND FALSE PROMISES

Todd A. DeMitchell
Richard Fossey

TECHNOMIC
PUBLISHING CO., INC.

LANCASTER · BASEL

The Limits of Law-Based School Reform
a **TECHNOMIC**®publication

Published in the Western Hemisphere by
Technomic Publishing Company, Inc.
851 New Holland Avenue, Box 3535
Lancaster, Pennsylvania 17604 U.S.A.

Distributed in the Rest of the World by
Technomic Publishing AG
Missionsstrasse 44
CH-4055 Basel, Switzerland

Printed in the United States of America
10 9 8 7 6 5 4 3 2 1

Main entry under title:
    The Limits of Law-Based School Reform: Vain Hopes and False Promises

A Technomic Publishing Company book
Bibliography: p.
Includes index p. 199

Library of Congress Catalog Card No. 96-61338
ISBN No. 1-56676-482-3

To Terri and Kim
Our Inspirations

CONTENTS

THE LIMITS OF LAW-BASED SCHOOL REFORM

Over the past twenty years, public education has been engaged in strenuous and highly public efforts to reform schooling. Although these reform efforts have varied widely in focus and philosophy, they all have had one thing in common. Every reform has been implemented through a legal initiative. State laws, school board policies, court decisions, and collective bargaining provisions have been the means by which school reform efforts have been defined, altered, and put into place.

Although the law has been the vehicle for launching school reform efforts, little attention has been paid to the way legal mechanisms enable and constrain effective school reform. For example, several state legislatures have attempted to empower teachers and create collegial school environments by passing laws that require school districts to implement site-based management. However, other laws—specifically state collective bargaining statutes—virtually mandate that teachers and school districts relate to one another as adversaries. Thus far, no state legislature has come to terms with this incongruity. Thus, in state after state, laws that mandate a collegial and cooperative work environment exist side by side with labor laws that make this worthy reform goal very difficult to attain.

Likewise, school reform advocates sometimes forget that ''Heaven is in the details'' when it comes to bringing about change. More than thirty states have passed some kind of school choice law that suggests radical changes in the relationship between schools and their clients; yet when these laws are analyzed, it becomes clear that school choice initiatives were drafted in such a way as to have minimum impact on established educational interests. Far from being revolutionary changes in the way educational services are delivered, these laws merely tinker with the status quo. Often, these reforms become mere window dressing designed to keep public scrutiny at bay.

Public education was created by laws, and laws are absolutely essential for pubic education to function efficiently and equitably in our large and diverse society. Without question, we need legal instruments, courts, and court-like mechanisms to provide effective education programs to the nation's 50 million school children. Nevertheless, legalization in its most virulent form becomes legalism. When this occurs, "law and procedures become ends in themselves and substantive goals are lost in mechanical adherence to form" (Neal & Kirp, 1986, p. 344). Even when legalization does not devolve into legalism, the inability of legal mechanisms to bring about mandated outcomes results in "tightening enforcement, increasing accountability, or clarifying guidelines" (Berman, 1986, p. 60). In other words, bureaucratic control increases. Legal mandates may be effective at prohibiting actions, but they typically are poor at facilitating the adoption of new behavior, attitudes, and beliefs—the core of true educational reform. As Berman (1986) writes, "Legalization and reform. These words fit uncomfortably together" (p. 46).

In the final analysis, laws, rules, and collective bargaining contracts can shape the structure of education, but they have a limited impact on the shared values of an institution or the core of teaching and learning—the very heart of education. Laws cannot dictate the way children are nurtured, nor can they create supportive learning environments. As Fullan (1993) writes, "structural changes are not sufficient without 'changes in ideas, beliefs, and attitudes' " (p. 78). Bureaucratic reform—rules or regulations—will fail without a corresponding concern for the way the culture of the school affects teaching and learning. Just having a law, rule, or regulation is not enough.

Furthermore, laws and law-like mechanisms are usually introduced to reduce conflict and foster stability. School reform advocates who rely solely on laws to improve education often fail to recognize that conflict and fluidity are frequently a necessary part of change. Stacey (1992) writes: "People spark new ideas off each other when they disagree—when they are conflicting, confused, and searching for new meaning—yet remain willing to discuss and listen to each other" (p. 120). Similarly,

Fullan (1993) posits that "problems are the route to deeper change" and "smoothness in the early stages of a change effort is a sure sign that superficial or trivial change is being substituted for substantial change attempts" (p. 26).

The subject of this book concerns the limitations of law as a means of improving the way the nation's children are educated. Chapters 3, 6, and 8 are based upon articles that appeared in the *International Journal of Educational Reform* (published by Technomic Publishing Co., Inc.). The volume is divided into four parts, with each part dedicated to a specific limitation of law-based school reform. These four sections are preceded by an overview chapter setting forth the history of school reform over the past two decades.

The first section, entitled "From a Distance, You Look Like a Friend: Collegiality and Unionism in the Schools" explores how unions and collective bargaining, in their current forms, are a hindrance to school reform. In these chapters, we point out that two decades of school reform have left an adversarial and dysfunctional model of labor relations, not only intact, but deeply entrenched. How, one of the chapters asks, can site-based management, with its promise of shared decision making and collegiality, be successful in a collective bargaining environment where teachers and school administrators are enemies almost by definition?

In the second part, entitled "Accountability Mechanisms: Inside and Outside the Classroom," we examine some of the legal mechanisms that hold the teaching profession accountable in some fashion to the public it is supposed to serve. The first chapter in this section asks the important question: "Who shall teach our children?" To whom are teachers accountable, and what aspects of teachers' lives are proper subjects for public scrutiny? This chapter looks at the dynamic tension that exists between the teaching profession and the larger community over who has final authority for deciding professional standards. This discussion is fundamental to education reform because no reform can be successful unless the person who stands at the front of the classroom is a skilled and dedicated professional.

The second chapter in this section revisits the old question of who is accountable for educating children. It examines the doctrine of educational malpractice in light of expanding research on the connection between professional practice and student outcomes.

The third section of the book is called "Classroom or Workplace:

Whose Place Is It?'' It asks whether schools are ultimately designed to be workplaces for the benefit of adults or learning places where students' needs come first.

The first chapter in this section outlines the way teachers' job protection rights often outweigh students' interests. A second chapter discusses the inadequacy of legal remedies for sexual abuse in the schools, where adults' legal rights often take precedence over children's safety.

The fourth part of the book is entitled ''Litigation and Legislation: In Dubious Battle for Reform.'' This section discusses the limitations of laws, courts, and legislatures in improving conditions in the nation's schools. In this section, we review three major legal reform initiatives — school desegregation litigation, beginning with *Brown v. Board of Education* (1954); the school funding lawsuits, designed to ensure equitable school funding, which now span almost three decades of litigation; and the charter school law movement, which has swept through numerous state legislatures beginning in the late 1980s. We also review a trend in the courts to restrict the first amendment rights of teachers while they are in their classrooms, a trend that may counteract legislative efforts to give teachers more autonomy.

This book's overarching theme is this: law-based school reforms — lawsuits, regulations, statutes, and collective bargaining provisions — have not changed the fundamental character of the nation's schools. Although hundreds of law-based reform initiatives have been introduced, most have had little effect on learning (Fuhrman et al., 1993). By themselves, law-based reform efforts offer the false promise of real change.

In our last chapter, we look beyond law-based school reform as the way to improve our children's future. Law-based reform is an important and necessary strategy, but by itself, it is inadequate to change the way children are schooled. Just as Virgil could go only so far toward taking Dante to paradise, rational decision making, which undergirds most law-based reform, can take us only partway to the schools our children deserve. School leaders must use both their heads and their hearts to improve education. Our book discusses the limits of the head. We hope it leads to an expanding dialogue on the nature of reform, a dialogue that infuses dimensions of the heart, the ''deeper and more enduring elements of courage, spirit, and hope'' (Bolman & Deal, 1995, p. 5) that so often go unspoken in our discussions of school reform.

REFERENCES

Berman, P. (1986). From compliance to learning: Implementing legally-induced reform. In D. L. Kirp and D. N. Jensen (Eds.). *School days, rule days: The legalization and regulation of education.* Philadelphia: Falmer Press.

Bolman, L. G. and Deal, T. E. (1995). *Leading with soul: An uncommon journey of the spirit.* San Francisco: Jossey-Bass.

Brown v. Board of Education, 347 U.S. 483 (1954).

Fuhrman, S. H., Elmore, R. F., and Massell, D. (1993). In S. L. Jacobson and R. Berne (Eds.). *Reforming education: The emerging systemic approach* (pp. 3–27). Thousand Oaks, CA: Corwin Press.

Fullan, M. (1993). *Change forces: Probing the depths of educational reform.* New York: Falmer Press.

Neal, D. and Kirp, D. L. 1986. The allure of legalization reconsidered: The case of special education. In D. L. Kirp and D. N. Jensen (Eds.). *School days, rule days: The legalization and regulation of education.* Philadelphia: Falmer Press.

Stacey, R. 1992. *Managing the unknowable.* San Francisco: Jossey-Bass Publishers.

CHAPTER 1

Reform: Legal Challenges Past and Present

> *Reform must focus not just on structure, policy, and regulations but on deeper issues of the culture of the system.*
>
> —Fullan & Miles (1992)

Education is no stranger to reform. Elmore and McLaughlin (1988) write: ''The history of American education is, in large part, the history of reform, or rather of recurring cycles of reform'' (p. 1). Reform is a recurring theme because education is of such importance to American society. Dialogue and debate about the goals of public education are a ''potent means of defining the present and shaping the future''; it is ''one way that Americans make sense of their lives'' (Tyack & Cuban, 1995, p. 42).

REFORM IN TWO MOVEMENTS

True to form, in the last decade, education has been involved in yet another reform movement. The fact that education is involved in a reform effort is not particularly momentous. Rather, what makes this reform different is the pervasiveness of the reform initiatives and the range of participants (National Governor's Conference, President Bush's education summit, the professional associations, America 2000, and many state legislatures, to name a few). Murphy (1989) notes that the scope and momentum of the movement are unparalleled. ''The attack

1

on a host of problems has been more comprehensive, of greater concentrated intensity, and has spawned more activity than at any other time in the past'' (p. 214). In short, the latest cycle of reform has been a time of unprecedented education policymaking.

Interestingly, the present reform movement was initiated by businesspeople and governmental actors, not educators. It was characterized by a top-down strategy, with the state being at the top and the classroom at the bottom. "State level action was comprehensive in tightening the system, but worked largely within the traditional structure of American public education" (Educational Testing Service, 1993, p. 85). Reform measures typically took the form of state mandates that increased the bureaucratic control of education. Often, the focus of this increased regulation was academic content and the implementation of higher standards for teachers and students (Elmore, 1990). Accountability was the buzzword at this time. These reforms included such initiatives as teacher testing, added instructional time, statewide assessment programs, heightened graduation requirements, and revised teacher certification standards.

The reform movement has been likened to two waves crashing on the shore of U.S. public education. The first wave focused on academic content and higher performance standards for teachers and students. The reforms of this wave originated primarily at the state level— through the actions of legislatures, policy makers, and governors. This reform wave generated more rules and regulations about education by the states than the previous twenty years had generated. Timar and Kirp (1988) estimated that over 700 statutes affecting some aspect of the teaching profession were enacted nationally from approximately 1986 to 1988.

The centralization of authority gained support from state policy makers who pursued school improvement through legislation (Cuban, 1990). The first wave of reform created a whole new body of rules, fostering the growth of bureaucracies to enforce those rules. For example, high school graduation requirements were raised in forty-two states. By 1990, forty-seven states had instituted statewide student testing programs, and thirty-nine states had increased teacher credentialing standards by mandating some form of teacher testing (Educational Testing Service, 1993).

During the first reform wave, many states enacted sweeping changes in their education codes, often in response to a deluge of reform reports.

For example, George Deukmejiian, governor of California, signed into law an omnibus education bill in 1983. This major reform law made more than eighty changes in the education code. Its initiatives included a mentor teacher program, incentives to lengthen the school day and school year, higher starting salaries for teachers, and the installation of an accountability program using the California Assessment Program's multiple matrix test. Similarly, in 1983 and 1984, Florida enacted legislation that introduced curriculum reform, tougher graduation requirements, specific performance standards, and an extended school day and school year.

This first wave of reform has been characterized as emphasizing excellence in education (First, 1992). It was "designed to focus public education on academic content and to introduce higher standards for students and teachers" (Elmore, 1990, p. 1). As seen in California and Florida and as we will see in Tennessee, the first wave involved upgrading the curriculum, establishing higher standards, and instituting achievement testing. States took the lead role in this wave and upstaged the professionals, their associations, and the local school boards (Table 1.1). Since the state was the central actor, the result was greater centralization, regulation, and bureaucratization of education.

As the states moved center stage in the theater of reform, they utilized four generic classes of policy instruments to "translate substantive policy goals (e.g., improved student achievement, higher quality entering teachers) into concrete actions" (McDonnell & Elmore, 1987, p. 134). According to McDonnell and Elmore (p. 134), these four alternative policy instruments are as follows:

- Mandates are rules governing the action of individuals and agencies and are intended to produce compliance.
- Inducements transfer money to individuals or agencies in return for certain actions.
- Capacity building is the transfer of money for the purpose of investment in material, intellectual, or human resources.
- Systems changing transfers official authority among individuals and agencies in order to alter the system by which public goods and services are delivered.

Applying the four alternative policy instruments to first wave reform efforts, it can be seen that the first wave primarily relied on

TABLE 1.1 Major state reform initiatives.

Reform	Enacted	Under Consideration	Total
Career ladder/merit pay	14	24	38
Salary increase/new minimum	18	17	35
Teacher testing	29	10	39
Revise certification	28	16	44
Revise teacher training	19	10	29
Aid prospective teachers	24	13	37
Add instructional time	13	7	20
Restrict extracurricular activities	6	4	10
Reduce class size	13	7	20
Raise graduation requirements	43	5	48
Require exit tests	15	4	19
Statewide assessment	37	6	43
Test for promotion	8	3	11
Increase college admission requirements	17	3	20
Academic recognition programs	25	5	30
Academic enrichment programs	34	8	42
State mandated discipline policy	19	8	27
Professional development for teachers	30	14	44
Professional development for administrators	30	12	42

Source: U.S. Department of Education, *Education Week* (June 2, 1984). Cited in Timar and Kirp, 1988, p. 13.

mandates (e.g., revising certification and teacher training, statewide assessment, raising graduation requirements) and inducements (e.g., career ladders, salary increases). Capacity building was used significantly less and systems-changing mechanisms were virtually nonexistent. Capacity building has distant effects focusing on future returns, while mandates and inducements produce proximate and tangible effects (McDonnell & Elmore, 1987). Since the trend was toward greater state control, it is easy to see why mandate and inducement policy instruments were chosen: they were short-term, visible, and thus more politically expedient. They maintained power at the state level, instead of transferring it, as systems-changing mechanisms would have done. The virtual lack of systems-changing policy mechanisms helped lead, or at least foreshadow, the second wave of reform.

The hope of the first wave of reform turned to criticism when its attendant rules, mandates, and monitoring did not achieve excellence.

Timar and Kirp (1988) commented that "the critical question that state reform efforts raise is whether reform policies yield outcomes that are consistent with standards of excellence, or whether reforms lead only to more rules, formalistic compliance, evasion, paperwork, and legal proceedings" (p. 5). Fullan (in Fullan with Steigelbauer, 1991), the noted expert on the change process, answered, "Regulatory approaches cannot accomplish reform" (p. 270). Mandates and incentives appeared to be left behind during the postmortem on the first wave. A second wave soon began to gather strength. It changed the policy instrument means of system changing to a policy objective generally called restructuring.

This first spate of reform ideas with their attendant initiatives and dialogue lasted a few scant years. Then, "with remarkable swiftness, the debate over how to reform public education shifted from strategies that would have strengthened the bureaucratic controls over teachers to strategies meant to 'empower them' " (Bacharach & Shedd, 1989, p. 148). The second group of reform reports issued by commissions from business, education, and statewide policy groups called for "major changes in the ways schools go about their work and the ways teachers are involved in their decision-making structure" (Lieberman et al., 1988, p. 148).

Linda Darling-Hammond (1988) noted that the "new" reformers argued that decisions about education must be professionalized and decentralized. In other words, the work of the first wave of reform must largely be undone. Instead of a top-down approach, reform must proceed from the bottom-up. Education had to be completely rebuilt, second wave reformers argued, not merely tinkered with. The call was to break the mold of education and build a new one.

This reconceptualization strove to professionalize teachers' work and status by altering the governance pattern of schools. By transferring the locus of decision making to the local school site and utilizing the professional expertise of teachers in the decision-making process, the second wave of reform hoped to improve schools by "empowering teachers rather than managing them" (Johnson, 1989, p. 95). "Teachers would assume responsibility for licensing and supervising their peers; they would exercise control over their classrooms and schools" (Johnson, 1989, p. 95).

In short, the second reform way was a movement away from regulatory control to professional and democratic control of individual schools. Second wave reformers and their commentators assumed that lasting school improvement would occur when teachers are accorded the autonomy to be professional decision makers at the school site (Carnegie Forum, 1986; Hallinger & Richardson, 1988; Johnson, 1990).

This second wave of reform looked at transforming the educational system and not just tinkering with it one piece at a time. The term *restructure* in many ways captured the essence of the second round of reform reports that supplied the intellectual and philosophical basis of the second wave. Restructuring loosely meant empowering teachers and principals by shifting and altering authority for decision making. Restructuring meant changing the organization and management of schools (Elmore, 1990) through decentralization and shifting the locus of management to the school site. Contrary to the first wave, which increased regulations, the second wave emphasized fewer regulations and less bureaucracy. The second wave was a push for greater professional control of education. Restructuring was viewed as "trading off increased decision-making authority for educators in exchange for both significant improvements in and accountability for student performance" (Cohen, 1990, p. 251). Restructuring broadened the "narrow" first wave focus on academics and teaching. Academics was redefined as success for all students. Equity seemed to reclaim its place of value next to the first wave's exhaltation of excellence.[1]

With the second wave surging up the shore of education, it is worthwhile to briefly visit the forces of change and one state's response to the siren call for reform.

THE NATURE OF CHANGE AND THE TENNESSEE EDUCATIONAL IMPROVEMENT ACT

It was against the backdrop of the second wave of reform that Ned McWherter, governor of Tennessee, on March 11, 1992, signed into law House Bill No. 752, commonly called The Educational Improvement Act. Tennessee had passed The Comprehensive Education Reform Act during the first wave of reform. And then, in 1992, it rode the second wave of reform with The Educational Improvement Act (TEIA).

House Bill No. 752 was an extensive piece of reform legislation. It had ninety sections, which impacted everything from the funding structure of education to the selection of superintendents. The new law included class size restrictions and a performance accountability system that estimated the effects of teacher, school, and district on educational outcomes. In addition, the legislation established family resource centers and changed the way high school students were tracked. "This goes all the way from the classroom to the board room," said Commissioner of Education Charles O. Smith. "It will affect everyone" (Harp, 1992). It was a far-reaching piece of legislation reminiscent of many first wave reforms with some second wave twists.

Before taking a closer look at Tennessee's reform act, it is worthwhile to take a short detour and review the change process. This is important because reform legislation is obviously meant to be implemented, thus altering the process of education in some manner so that desired outcomes can be met. Education reform is meant to bring about change. Fullan and Miles (1992), in a *Phi Delta Kappan* article, raised a cautionary note about reform. They wrote, "Wishful thinking and legislation have poor records as tools for social betterment" (p. 752). If they are correct (and we think they are concerning legislation), knowledge about the change process can inform policymaking and policy implementation.

Mandates, rules, and regulations are not enough if reform efforts are to be effective and not fall prey to the issue-attention cycle that has claimed many reforms. Fullan (in Fullan with Steigelbauer, 1991), in his analysis of the role of governments in the change process, concludes that "the appropriate model for change is not an innovation, but rather an institutional capacity or developmental model" (p. 267). This would seem to indicate that capacity-building policy instruments may be the more effective alternative to mandates in the long run. In addition, he strongly suggests that high regulation and high monitoring can achieve minimal compliance at best and that the key to real reform is found in "low to medium regulation (guidelines more than prescriptions), combined with high engagement (negotiation, technical assistance, monitoring, feedback, problem solving)" (p. 270).

The components of The Educational Improvement Act are too numerous to discuss in depth in this space. Table 1.2 briefly describes the reform, the policy mechanism used for implementation, and the reform wave that best fits a particular initiative. The decision about which policy mechanism and which wave is most appropriate is based on the previous discussion and the best estimate given that a choice must

TABLE 1.2 *Selected reform programs from Tennessee.*

Program	Policy Mechanism	Wave
Basic Education Program		
New funding plan intended to bring equity to districts	Mandate	2nd
$200 provided for every teacher for instructional supplies	Capacity building	2nd
Funding for duty-free lunch for teachers	Mandate	2nd
Implement the K–3 at-risk class size program	Mandate	2nd
Management Information System	Mandate	1st
Performance goals for all districts to be established—probation required for noncompliance	Mandate	2nd
Value-added assessment for estimating teacher, school, and district effects on student outcomes	Mandate	2nd
Commissioner's Annual Report	Mandate	1st
County Superintendent Selected for up to 4-Year Contract	Mandate	2nd
Power to dismiss employees	Mandate	2nd
Power to employ principals	Mandate	2nd
School-Based Decision Making	Systems changing	2nd
Local boards may initiate programs		
Graduation Requirements	Mandate	1st
Class Size	Mandate	1st
Established average class size per school with maximums for individual classes		
Contingent on full funding for BEP		
Boards of Education	Mandate	2nd
Elected		
Ungraded/Unstructured Classes	Systems changing	1st
Allows local boards to experiment without loss of BEP funding		
Office of Educational Accountability	Mandate	1st
Monitor performance of school boards, superintendents, school districts, schools, and school personnel		
Waiver of School Fees	Mandate	2nd
School fees are waived for students who receive free or reduced school lunches		

TABLE 1.2 (continued).

Program	Policy Mechanism	Wave
Unification Educational Planning Commission The Commission shall study the need for consolidation of all county schools into a unified school system.	Systems changing	2nd
Credentialing Program for Principals	Mandate	2nd
Family Resource Center Family resource centers may be established to meet the needs of families with children. Centers are to be located in or near a school $50,000 grants are available for planning the center	Capacity building	2nd
Alternative Educational Program $50,000 grants awarded to eight school systems to support alternative education, which emphasizes school-based decision making	Capacity building	2nd
Break-the-Mold Schools An unspecified fund is available for break-the-mold schools Break-the-Mold schools are exempt from the roles or regulations regulations or policies of either the state board of education or the local board of education	Systems changing	2nd
Choice A window of opportunity is created in which school boards may admit pupils from other districts without the approval of the former district.	Systems changing	2nd

Source: DeMitchell, 1992, p. 414.

be made. Some readers may disagree, but then the ensuing discussion would be beneficial in understanding the complex forces at work in reform movements.

As can be readily seen from Table 1.2, the Tennessee Educational Improvement Act is extensive. It focused its choice of policy mechanisms (two-thirds of the reforms cited) on mandates, while the majority of reforms appear to be clustered in the second wave of reform. Many of the reforms are reminiscent of the first wave reforms. In other words, many of the law's reform initiatives tended to be bureaucratic in nature (the Office of Educational Accountability, for example). This facet of Tennessee school reform appears to be at odds with its neighboring state's (Kentucky) attack on bureaucracy. Indeed, Kentucky abolished the state department of education for a time as part of its reform package.

Another point illustrated by Table 1.2 is this: Although the Educational Improvement Act was created during the second wave of reform, some of its programs are more closely aligned with first wave reforms. The Act, as already noted, used mandates, a mechanism often associated with the first wave, as the principal way to improve public education in the state. This suggests that it may be misleading to describe reform packages as either first wave or second wave. It may be more accurate to say that reform ideologies can be characterized as separate waves only because of their placement in time. In fact, reform legislation might better be described as tidal, with various reform strategies ebbing and flowing as they react to the strong gravitational pull of competing ideologies. A tidal metaphor may also be a more apt description than a wave because most pieces of reform legislation lack the cohesiveness necessary to keep a distinct wave from disintegrating into the choppy water of conflicting reform philosophies (DeMitchell, 1992).

A LEGAL CHALLENGE UNMET IN
OCEAN HILL-BROWNSVILLE

The potential for legal challenges of reform efforts is formidable. A brief review of history underscores this need for discussion on the legal challenges of reform. Tyack and Cuban (1995), in their thoughtful book *Tinkering toward Utopia: A Century of Public School Reform,* note that educational reformers are captives of history. ''Whether they are aware of it or not, all people use history (defined as an interpretation of past events) when they make choices about the present and future. The issue is not whether people use a sense of the past in shaping their lives but how accurate and appropriate are their historical maps'' (p. 6). As fellow captives, we offer the story of Ocean Hill-Brownsville as a historical map of the legal challenges of reform.

In 1967, with the help of the Ford Foundation, three decentralization projects were initiated in the sprawling New York City Schools. The Ford Foundation provided seed money for three demonstration projects in three of New York's local districts. At the press conference announcing the grants, the disparity between what the board of education thought it had authorized and what the community groups expected became apparent (Ravitch, 1974). In one demonstration district—the Ocean Hill-Brownsville District—this misunderstanding led to considerable problems, ultimately resulting in the shutdown of the entire New York City School system by a teacher strike.

The proposed governing board for each demonstration district consisted of four community members, eight parents, four teachers, and one supervisor. Disagreements on the board were to be resolved by consensus. The governing board was given the authority to choose a chief administrator and a principal, set educational standards, and develop curriculum. The governing boards did not have the power to hire and fire teachers. The contract with the teachers and their union was not abrogated by the establishment of the demonstration districts. As Diane Ravitch observed about the decentralization plan, "It was a plan for community participation, not a plan for community control" (Ravitch, 1974, p. 321). At least, that is what the board of education of the New York City School District intended.

After implementing the decentralization plan, the governing board of Ocean Hill-Brownsville came to the conclusion that the problems it was experiencing with its professional staff could not be solved unless the community gained greater control of the schools. In 1968, the Ocean Hill-Brownsville board, along with boards in the other two demonstration districts, prepared a document listing the powers they thought were necessary to achieve more local control. Some of the powers sought were total control of all money, the power to hire and fire all personnel, the power to negotiate with the teachers' union, and the power to contract for building and rehabilitation of individual schools.

For the New York City Board of Education, the demonstration boards' demands for control were problematic. The board of education could not legally delegate the powers that the demonstration boards had sought, yet the governing boards believed that they could not succeed unless they received all the additional powers outlined in their document.

Soon a dispute arose between the Ocean Hill-Brownsville governing board and New York City's teachers' union after the board removed nineteen professionals from their positions for the upcoming school year without the benefit of due process. The governing board vowed that the ousted personnel would never enter its schools again. The teachers' union was equally determined that its members wouuld return to the classroom.

The stage was set for a confrontation, and several hundred police were called in to keep order. At one point, the governing board closed its schools, and when the schools were reopened, 300 to 350 teachers walked out on strike. The governing board hired 350 teachers during the summer to replace all of the teachers who went out on strike.

The next September, when schools were set to reopen, the teachers' union went out on strike several times, at one point shutting down the entire New York City school system. On one occasion, disorder broke out in the streets, with several hundred community members battling the police. At several schools, students were led out of their class by the replacement teachers in protest against returning union teachers.

Not all attempts at restructuring have had such an extreme result. But there is a lesson in the Ocean Hill-Brownsville confrontation. Diane Ravitch, in *The Great School Wars* (1974), wrote: "In retrospect, it was clear that the Board of Education had erred in permitting the projects to get underway before establishing concise descriptions of the powers that would be granted to [the demonstration projects] and the powers that would not and could not . . ." (1974, p. 357).

At its heart, the dispute in Ocean Hill-Brownsville involved legal issues. Specifically, the powers sought by the governing board—authority over personnel and budget—were powers already designated by New York law and collective bargaining contracts. These are two of the same powers that are thought today to be necessary for achieving effective site-based management, one of the central initiatives of the second reform wave. The actions of the Ocean Hill-Brownsville board and its collaborators were a reaction to bureaucratic control buttressed by legalization. Nevertheless, the board failed to fully understand the legal constraints that ultimately doomed its reform initiatives to failure.

As Sykes and Elmore (1989) observed, "The prevailing tendency in educational policy and administrative practice today is to create rules, structures and routines that increase compliance as they impoverish education" (p. 92). The tendency toward legalization is evident, but its descendence into legalism is not. Clearly, the legal climate that schools operate in is an important reform consideration, one that must be understood and addressed but is often left unattended.

The legal challenges of reform are formidable but not necessarily insurmountable; vain hopes and false promises of law-based reform is not the necessary outcome of all reform efforts. Nevertheless, legal issues, as the Ocean Hill-Brownsville conflict illustrates, must be identified prior to implementing fundamental reforms, such as changes in school governance. Failure to forge a formal understanding of the parameters and extent of authority in decision making is to court disaster. Certain basic legal issues cannot remain unresolved while restructuring projects are underway. To give educational reforms the best possible chance of success, the legal challenges discussed in the following sections must be confronted and overcome.

REFERENCES

Bacharach, S. B. and Shedd, J. B. (1989). Power and empowerment: The constraining myths and emerging structures of teacher unionism in an age of reform. In J. Hannaway and R. Crowson (Eds.) *The politics of reforming school administration*. New York: Falmer Press.

Carnegie Forum on Education and the Economy. (1986, May). *A nation prepared: Teachers for the 21st century.* Washington, D.C.

Cohen, M. (1990). Key issues confronting state policymakers. In R. F. Elmore and Associates. *Restructuring schools: The next generation of educational reform.* San Francisco: Jossey-Bass.

Cuban, L. (1990). Reforming again, again, and again. *Educational Researcher* 19(1): 3 – 13.

Darling-Hammond, L. (1988). Policy and professionalism. In A. Lieberman (Ed.) *Building a professional culture in schools.* New York: Teachers College Press.

DeMitchell, T. A. (1992). The Tennessee Educational Improvement Act: A beginning discussion. *International Journal of Educational Reform* 1:412 – 418.

Educational Testing Service (1993). *Education Issues of the 1990s.* Princeton, NJ: Policy Information Center.

Elmore, R. F. (1990). Introduction: On changing the structure of public schools. In R. F. Elmore and Associates (Eds.) Restructuring schools: The next generation of educational reform. San Francisco: Jossey-Bass.

Elmore, R. F. and McLaughlin, M. W. (1988). *Steady work: Policy, practice, and the reform of American education.* Santa Monica, CA: Rand.

First, P. (1992). *Educational policy for school administrators.* Boston: Allyn and Bacon.

Floden, R. E., Goertz, M. E., and O'Day, J. (1995). Capacity building in systemic reform. *Phi Delta Kappan* 77(1):19 – 21.

Fullan, M. G. with Steigelbauer, S. (1991). *The new meaning of change,* second edition. New York: Teachers College Press.

Fullan, M. G. and Miles, M. B. (1992). Getting reform right: What works and what doesn't. *Phi Delta Kappan,* 73(10):745 – 752.

Fuhrman, S. H., Elmore, R. F., and Massell, D. (1993). School reform in the United States: Putting it in context. In S. L. Jacobson and R. Berne (Eds.) *Reforming education: The emerging systemic approach.* Thousand Oaks, CA: Corwin Press.

Hallinger, P. and Richardson, D. (1988). Models of shared leadership: Evolving structures and relationships. *Urban Review* 20(4):229 – 245.

Harp, L. (1992, March 11). Tenn. governor to sign long-awaited school-reform bill. *Education Week.*

Johnson, S. M. (1989). Schoolwork and its reform. In J. Hannaway and R. Crowson (Eds.) *The politics of reforming school administration*. New York: Falmer Press.

Johnson, S. M. (1990). *Teachers at work: Achieving success in our schools*. New York: Basic Books.

Lieberman, A., Saxl, E. R., and Miles, M. B. (1988). Teacher leadership: Ideology and practice. In A. Lieberman (Ed.) *Building a professional culture in schools*. New York: Teachers College Press.

McDonnell, L. M. and Elmore, R. F. (1987). Getting the job done: Alternative policy instruments. *Educational Evaluation and Policy Analysis* 9:134.

Murphy, J. (1989). Educational reform in the 1980s: Explaining some surprising successes. *Educational Evaluation and Policy Analysis* 11(3):209–221.

Ravitch, D. (1974). *The great school wars*. New York: Basic Books.

Smith, M. S. and O'Day, J. (1991). Systemic school reform. In S. Fuhrman and B. Malen (Eds.) *The politics of curriculum and testing,* pp. 233–267. Bristol, PA: Falmer Press.

Sykes, T. B. and Elmore, R. F. (1989). Making school manageable. In J. Hannaway and R. Crowson (Eds.) *The politics of reforming school administration*. New York: The Falmer Press.

Timar, T. B. and Kirp, D. L. (1988). *Managing educational excellence*. New York: Falmer Press.

Tyack, D. and Cuban, L. (1995). *Tinkering toward utopia: A century of public school reform*. Cambridge, MA: Harvard University Press.

ENDNOTE

1. The reform efforts of the first and second waves of reform were broad, but evidence suggests that they have been shallow in their effects (Fuhrman et al., 1993). Some commentators have remarked that, possibly, because of the failure of the first two waves to make second-order changes in the schools, a third wave has formed. This third wave combines the first two waves in an effort to achieve coordination and coherence. Coherence in the educational system is achieved through centralized coordination and increased professional discretion at the school site around a clear set of definitions of what is a thoughtful, competent, and responsible citizen (Smith & O'Day, 1991). Some researchers and policy makers are advocating for capacity building as the mechanism of choice in the third wave (Floden et al., 1995).

PART ONE

FROM A DISTANCE, YOU LOOK LIKE A FRIEND: COLLEGIALITY AND UNIONISM IN THE SCHOOLS

CHAPTER 2

Teachers' Unions: Barrier or Vehicle for Reform?

> *Al Shanker, the president of the American Federation of Teachers, warned teachers at a union convention in Niagara Falls in 1985 that "we have not been able to achieve all that we had hoped for through the bargaining process, and it is time to do something additional and quite different."*
>
> — quoted in Toch, 1991, p. 134

Teachers' unions are major players in public education today. Kerchner and Mitchell (1988) consider the unionization of public school teachers to be one of the three most influential structural changes impacting the governance of America's public schools that has occurred since the end of World War II. (See Table 2.1 for the relative clout of teachers' unions.) The power and influence of the unions is chiefly attained and exerted through public sector collective bargaining laws. Thirty-four states have public employee collective bargaining laws, and nine additional states either give school districts the discretion to bargain or require consultation between the school districts and their unions. Any proposed reform strategies that affect the terms and working conditions of unionized employees must be bargained for in those schools that have collective bargaining. Since any meaningful change in schools must affect teachers' work, any significant reform efforts must intersect the business of unions.

Public sector collective bargaining is a creature of state legislation. Collective bargaining focuses on the rights of the workers (wages,

17

TABLE 2.1 Policy influential groups.

(25)					
••					
••					
••					
••		(16)			
••		••			
••		••			
••		••			
••		••			
••		••			
••	(5)	••			
••	••	(2)	••	(1)	(3)
••	••	••	••	••	••
Teacher Unions	School Boards Assoc.	School Administrators Assoc.	State Education Departments	PTA	Other Citizen Groups

Education Week (September 28, 1994, p. 30) conducted an informal telephone survey of sources in state legislature committees and governors' offices to determine which education groups have the most influence in shaping educational policy. Listed is an abbreviation of the results as to which group is perceived as having the most clout over educational policy issues. It represents how many times each group was rated as being the most influential.

terms, and conditions of employment), uses legal concepts and techniques to frame the rights (the negotiated contract), and lastly, utilizes court-like procedures to enforce and protect those rights (grievances, arbitration, and unfair labor practice charges).

Since collective bargaining is an aspect of legalization, one of the basic issues facing unions and collective bargaining is whether collective bargaining has descended into legalism where compliance with the contract becomes an end in itself. Cresswell and Murphy (1980) comment that collective bargaining is an arena in which rules themselves may undergo goal displacement, becoming ends rather than means – this is a chief characteristic of legalism. Has collective bargaining lost touch with the public policy goal that spawned its creation, of achieving labor peace so as to better insure the efficient, effective, uninterrupted delivery of educational services to the community? Some assert yes as the answer.

Lieberman (1984) argues that "teacher unions and teacher bargaining either frustrates most reforms or would be sufficient to frustrate them regardless of the presence or absence of other barriers to reform" (p. 54). Mitchell (1986) asserts that collective bargaining has not worked out the way its advocates once hoped. In a review of reform components, DeMitchell (1993) noted that "collective bargaining, as it is currently practiced in our school districts, is not up to the challenges posed by the reform goals of professionalizing the teaching work force and restructuring schools" (p. 78). In a similar vein, Johnson (1987) commented that collective bargaining is a hindrance to the process of designing new programs and resolving difficult problems such as collegial responsibility or pedagogical technique. Wise, in *Legislated Learning* (1979), argued that indivdually, faculty members resisted the forces associated with hyperrationalization by invoking their professionalism, but "collectively they may well contribute to them" (p. 103). In other words, unionization fostered more rules through the process of collective bargaining and the use of "legalistic procedures to limit administrator discretion" (p. 104), which in turn, limits professional autonomy, a goal of the second wave of reform. Fossey and Miles (1991), in a study of school-based management efforts in Boston's public schools, found that the relationship between the teacher's union and management hindered the effective implementation of this reform strategy in at least two important ways:

> First, restrictive contract language guards teachers' seniority at the expense of innovation at the school level. Second, grievances and arbitration decisions reinforce outmoded definitions of management and labor, discouraging a cooperative working relationship between teachers and administrators. (p. 4)

These commentators see collective bargaining or, maybe more broadly, unionism as a barrier to reform: both must be contended with, worked around, or altered to meet the needs of real systemic reform.

On the other hand, other observers of the reform landscape see unions and collective bargaining in a different light. Some (e.g., McDonnell & Pascall, 1988; Shedd & Bacharach, 1991) contend that neither the unions nor collective bargaining have been major obstacles to reform and may have strengthened school management. Not surprisingly, the two major teachers' unions maintain that greater professionalism for teachers can only be achieved through a strong negotiated contract. Supporters of collective bargaining as a vehicle for reform have pointed to the negotiated contracts in Toledo, Ohio; Dade County, Florida; and Rochester, New York, as examples of the way that the collective bargaining process can achieve the reform goals of professionalizing teachers' work in these districts, school boards and teachers' unions using collective bargaining to restructure governance patterns, and giving teachers some voice in the hiring and firing process. Koppich and Kerchner (1993), in a study of a dozen school districts that appear to have moved beyond old-style industrial unionism to professional unions, write: ''Collective bargaining and its outcome – the contract – thus become strategic tools in the battery of education reform techniques. Moreover, the contract itself recognizes the symbiotic connection, in a public enterprise, among union-management interaction, continuous school improvement, and obligations to the larger community'' (pp. 89 – 90). For example, in Glenview, Illinois, the teachers' union adopted a constitution which gave them a role in making educational decisions. The union president argued that ''the constitution allows teachers to focus on instruction and teaching without worrying about the details of a union contract'' (Checkley, 1996, p. 5).

This link between collective bargaining and the current reform agenda is particularly salient now (McDonnell & Pascal, 1988). Reform efforts must come to grips with unionism and collective bargaining. Neither can be ignored or wished away. A quick look at the historical roots that have shaped teacher unions and collective bargaining may be helpful as we wrestle with reform and the legalism of unions and collective bargaining.

INDUSTRIAL UNIONISM IN EDUCATION

Congress, in 1935, passed the National Labor Relations Act (NLRA) in an effort to safeguard workers' rights to organize and bargain collectively with their employer. This act created substantial rights for private sector employees but specifically excluded public employees from its protection. Bargaining rights for government employees progressed slowly, in part, because of the long-standing concern about the impact of public employees organizing on the ability of government to provide essential services and the use of private sector labor tactics such as a strike against the good of the public. Calvin Coolidge's response to the Boston police strike in 1919 struck a resonant chord with the nation, which lingered long after the strike was over. As the governor of Massachusetts, he stated that there was ''no right to strike against the public safety by anybody, anywhere, any time.''

Nevertheless, when public-sector collective bargaining laws were passed in the various states, starting in the 1960s, the predominant labor-management template that was used was that of the industrial unions. Thus, the labor relations model that had been adopted for the coal mine, the steel mill, and the auto plant was transferred to the school and the kindergarten classroom. This initial decision regarding what model to use for public sector labor law has had major consequences for education. Private sector industrial unionism, as codified in the NLRA, has several important components that exert a powerful influence over a teacher's work life and the operation of his or her school.

Streshly and DeMitchell (1994) note some of the ways that industrial unionism has shaped labor relations in our public schools:

- The union protects the worker from the whims of management through a collectively bargained, legally enforceable contract that establishes wages and benefits and defines the terms and conditions of employment in addition to the wages and benefits associated with the job.
- Employment security is obtained through due process procedures that protect employee rights while at the same time defining management responsibilities.
- There is an inherent separateness of labor and management in the industrial model. Consequently, teachers are labor, and administrators are managers. The fact that both groups are educators with common goals and values often gets lost. The separateness of some of the work activities performed by the teachers and the administrators is emphasized, and not the commonality of purpose, roots, interests, or overlapping functions.
- This separateness is strengthened in that you are either one or the other—teacher or manager. If you are a teacher, you can join the union; if you are not, you cannot. Union membership is exclusive. In legal terms, membership is based on a mutuality of interests of the employees. The mutuality of interests has little or nothing to do with the profession of education or the goals of an educational institution.
- ''Industrial unionism assumes permanent adversaries'' (Kerchner & Caufman, 1993, p. 15). An ''us'' and ''them'' mentality is fostered.
- Teachers' work is considered labor rather than a craft, an art, or a profession. The rich texture of a teacher's efforts, those professional and artistic elements, do not fit the industrial union model.

- "The value of laboring work is fixed by the *amounts* of work done in a unit of time, not by the level of skill or the capacity for judgment used by the workers" (Mitchell, 1986, p. 9, emphasis in original). An important industrial union principle is "equal pay for equal work"—and its corollary "extra pay for extra work" (Shedd & Bacharach, 1990). Whereas, professional associations and artistic unions, such as the Screen Writers Guild, "concentrate on guaranteeing the independence of workers and the *value* of the work they perform, rather than on employee rights" (Mitchell, 1986, p. 9).
- Collective bargaining is built around official bargaining teams where there is a "formal exchange of initial positions within a narrowly defined scope of bargaining" (Glaser, 1989, p. 33).
- The workers relinquish control over the outcome of the product of their work. Decisions about what is produced and how it is produced pass into the hands of management. The workers are divorced from the formation of policy; all they can do is

TABLE 2.2 Work structure to be supported.

	Labor	Craft	Profession	Art
Worker Organizations Emphasize:	Bargaining with management	Organizing workers	Certifying practitioners	Evaluating products
When they are empowered to:				
1. Define work based on:	Working conditions	Task definition	Public policy	Poduct distribution
2. Control worker access to:	Terms of employment	The guild	Client treatment	Specific jobs
3. Define membership based on	Employment	Apprenticeship	Examination and license	Recognition of talent
4. Give workers control by:	Limiting management rights	Expanding autonomy	High social status	Product ownership

>————————— MORE CONTROL OVER THE WORK ITSELF ————————>
<————————— MORE CONTROL OVER PRODUCTION PROCESSES ————————<

Source: Kerchner, C. T. & Mitchell, D. E. (1988). *The changing idea of a teachers' union.* New York: The Falmer Press.

implement it. For instance, in several states, the public employee collective bargaining law prohibits management from bargaining over matters of policy.

*   Industrial unionism tries to narrow the range of labor relations to only those items that are bargained. An often quoted union maxim is, "It isn't real if it isn't in the contract," and, if it is not in the contract, it is management's prerogative.
*   Work rules must be applied uniformly to all union members and all work sites. As applied to a school district, this concept means that the contract must be enforced and interpreted in the same way in all schools and situations. There can be no flexibility of circumstances or context. Uniformity is typically enforced by union officials and top-level management, thus increasing the centralizing of employee/employer decisions into the hands of a few.

Table 2.2 depicts the contrasting views of how work can be structured. The first category, labor, is indicative of the industrial union model.

THE WORK OF UNIONS AND THE NATURE OF COLLECTIVE BARGAINING

The work of unions points to the shortcomings of collective bargaining as a reform vehicle. McDonnell and Pascal (1988) have characterized the role of unions in the following manner:

> First, they operate as political interest groups, working to obtain benefits from the external environment. And, second they also function as voluntary organizations that must meet members' demands in the type and level of benefits they obtain and the services they provide. The challenge for the unions is to obtain sufficient benefits to maintain their membership, while also operating effectively in a world of political bargaining and compromise. (p. vii)

While it is true that unions play a prominent role in shaping policies that affect public schools, unions are empowered and exist to meet the self-interests of their members—not the interests of the general public. The elected school board is responsible for meeting the general social goals of an educated citizenry. The union's function is legally and psychologically distanced from the responsibility for the institution of education (Kerchner & Mitchell, 1988). Even though both the NEA and the AFT have stressed that teaching is a profession, their emphasis has been on attaining material benefits such as higher wages and better health insurance.

The importance of this central function of the union cannot be overstated. A Rand study (McDonnell & Pascal, 1988) found that "union efforts to obtain status benefits such as increased participation in school-site decision making often engenders teacher suspicion and a feeling that the union is 'falling down on the job.'" Until a "union obtains these bread-and-butter items, movement toward greater professionalism is not likely" (p. 53). Clearly, teachers expect their union to take care of business first, and the first business of a union is to secure the material benefits of their employment. A union official who strays too far from that prime directive does so at great peril to his or her position of leadership. Union reform efforts will, in all likelihood, be sacrificed whenever wages and benefits do not keep pace with the members' expectations.

In a five-state study of local school reform efforts and the impact of collective bargaining, DeMitchell and Barton (1994) found results similar to the McDonnell and Pascal (1988) study. The DeMitchell and Barton study surveyed the perceptions of the principal, union representative, and randomly selected teachers at 125 schools. A major focus of the study was the impact of collective bargaining on reform efforts at individual schools and the impact of collective bargaining on the quality of education that a school delivers. Not surprisingly, the study found that teachers were not aligned with their principals. However, what *was* surprising was the extent to which teachers also stood apart from their school's union representative. The study raises some questions about bargaining and school reform. The authors write: "A primary concern is 'Do teachers care about bargaining and reform?' Although the rise of unions and collective bargaining was built on a foundation of self-interest, that self-interest may not extend to professional activities. . . . Teachers may not see unions as being related to activities that are at the core of teaching" (pp. 26–27).

A second issue raised by the study is, "Who do union reps represent?" In response, the authors offer as part of their conclusion:

> There is some evidence in this study that union representatives are not necessarily speaking for their constituency of teachers but for the union as a separate entity. The moderate stances of teachers on issues regarding bargaining and reform are not apparent in the responses of their union

representatives. Nor do teachers seem to be polarized along the same lines that polarize the management-union debate. From their point of view, collective bargaining is neither an obstacle nor a vehicle for reform, it is neither positive nor negative, it is just irrelevant. (p. 27)

These two studies point out that the work of unions is often divorced from the real target of educational reform — interactions between teachers and students.

A second reason for skepticism about collective bargaining as a vehicle of reform is the process of collective bargaining as it is practiced in the vast majority of school districts throughout the nation. Collective bargaining, for several reasons is not working out the way its advocates had hoped (Mitchell, 1986). Many individuals have recognized the limitations of collective bargaining as a tool enabling educators to realize the goals of school reform. Its limited usefulness is due to several factors.

First, collective bargaining is an adversarial process. It takes the broader, inclusive concept of educator and sharply splits it into "us and them." It fosters a schism between teachers and administrators, a schism that restructuring seeks to repair. The reform goals of cohesion and collegiality are difficult to meet through collective bargaining. Schools need trust and cooperation to attain these goals. Collective bargaining is a system for creating agreement when trust is low. "As a consequence, contracts must be legally explicit, anticipate contingencies, and provide for policing and enforcement. Such a system may well exaggerate the differences and diminish trust between parties" (Cresswell & Murphy, 1980, p. 479).

The adversarial nature of bargaining is difficult to overcome long term, as well as short term. The Toledo teachers' union and the school system appeared to have overcome some of this adversarialness when they devised a first of its kind, peer review system in the 1980s. This program focused union efforts on the professional issue of only placing quality teachers in classrooms. Evaluation has long been the province of administration, with unions relegated to insuring due process procedures are strictly met. The Toledo Plan created a new relationship between the union and its members, a relationship where professional standards are enforced. In Toledo, teachers, through the intern-intervention program, used to evaluate and counsel teachers about their professional performance. Unfortunately in 1995, the program was scrapped by the Toledo Federation of Teachers "in a dispute with the school board over extra pay for principals" (Bradley, 1995, p. 3). The program fell prey to hardball bargaining when the school board refused to accept the demands of the union not to pay principals an extra stipend for administering a new state proficiency test. The teachers wanted the board to "postpone discussions of such extra pay until January, when all of its employee contracts expire" (Bradley, 1995, p. 3). The union retreated from a professional position regarding education to the old-style industrial union protectionist stance of its members. How many other reforms won at the bargaining table will be subjected to the ongoing pressure of bargaining tactics? Can a reform ever be institutionalized, or must it always be a chip to be dealt away at the bargaining table to achieve some other goal?

Second, bargaining is a rule-making activity that tends to entangle a school district, its schools, and its employees in an expanding web of rules. The negotiated contract is, in fact, a body of rules. A perusal of any contract will reveal section after section of rules governing all kinds of items – from how many days a teacher has to file a grievance to what constitutes a personal leave day. As such, it increases the number of rules under which teachers operate, thus reinforcing the bureaucratic tendency of the organization. What used to go on between the employee and the supervisor, or teacher and principal, is no longer just between those two. Their acts are now connected to others in a larger mosaic. "Collective bargaining has pushed for a more tightly coupled institution through a woven web of rules that increases uniformity" (Streshly & DeMitchell, 1994, p. 54).

The increase of bureaucratic rules to govern behavior supports a centralization of power. Since the contract is between the school board and the union, both parties are charged with its uniform application. Uniformity is enforced at the central office by both union and school district officials through the formal grievance process and the informal, and sometimes guarded, relationship that often develops between union officials and district office administrators. The contract seeks uniform application; since flexibility might lead to instability, which could endanger the labor peace achieved by the contract. Both the union and the district office administrators seek to centralize and standardize behavior through consistent rule interpretation, scrutiny, and enforcement.

The Boston schools is a prime example of how union work rules contributed to an inflexible environment for educating children. An event as important as a parent-teacher conference had to be scheduled 30 days in advance (Fossey & Miles, 1991). The desire to protect the "rights" of the teachers in this instance clearly came into conflict with the important function of parent-teacher communication. Rules such as these are indicative of industrial unionism and not a professional commitment to education.

In the end, the contract document itself becomes a symbol for the way teachers and administrators understand their daily work. The symbol of contracts as an important rule, if not the rule-making authority in schools, is seen in the size of the contract. Ultimately, it is the size of the pages, not the number of pages, that is the symbol of its power. Contracts are reduced in size so that they may be easily carried in one's shirt pocket or purse to be brandished as the final arbiter in educational disputes. To many, the contract defines the work of teaching, not the ethos of the profession, the wisdom of practice, or the research that informs practice. All too often, the contract, not the ethos of teaching, becomes the ultimate guide for a teacher's behavior.

This leads to the third factor, the contract language. Normative descriptions of work associated with professionalism do not easily translate into legalistic contrived contract clauses. Cohesion and collegiality cannot be mandated by a clause in a negotiated agreement.

Indeed, some common contract language operates in the opposite way by working against reform. Collective bargaining agreements, for example, often contain provisions that prevent the assignment of the most appropriate teacher to a school. Some view this as antithetical to professionalism (McDonnell & Pascal, 1988). In an analysis of Boston Public School's negotiated site-based management program, Richard Fossey and Karen Miles (1991) found that the emphasis on seniority "protected by the union contract and reinforced by several arbitration decisions hindered the ability of site administrators to reorganize their staffs to achieve economies or to institute innovative teaching programs" (p. 9). Other contract provisions that have been noted as problematic for reform include transfer policies that favor senior faculty members, limits on the number and length of faculty meetings, and mandated districtwide inservice policies that are inconsistent with reform's prescription that individual school staffs determine what inservice is most appropriate.

A word or two regarding the role of contract provisions and site-based management is in order at this point even though the whole issue of site-based management will be explored in greater depth in the next chapter. One of the major provisions, and a controversial one, of site-based management is the need for the site to be free from onerous school district regulations and union contract rules. Typically, there is an agreed upon process that allows a school to waive various portions of the contract that inhibit its ability to manage itself. This tenet recognizes that the centralizing and standardizing aspect of union contract enforcement runs counter to the need for flexibility. In other words, reform at the local level runs smack up against the contract. In order for the reform to take place the contract must yield. Waivers of contract provisions that are barriers to reform efforts are becoming more and more common.

For example, in Boston, in a trade of reforms for higher compensation (Canallos & Walker, 1993), the school committee and the union negotiated a pact in which six "explorer" schools would be created. These explorer schools would be exempt from all union rules. In other words, a contract was negotiated in which the contract has no power in order that reform can take place.

BEYOND THE CONTRACT

Reformers pushing for a more professional workplace and a decentralized school system must confront the fact that teacher unions are often a barrier to reform. This does not mean that teacher unions are the great horned devil of education. On the contrary, unions were created to solve a very real problem — how to protect teachers from arbitrary and capricious school boards and administrators.

Nevertheless, collective bargaining, as it is currently practiced, cannot bring the current reform agenda to fruition. There must be substantial changes if real reform is going to be achieved, and since unions are inextricably linked to the process of collective bargaining, a change in one will invariably necessitate a change in the other.

First, unions must rethink their role. Of course, the unions must continue to meet the bread-and-butter issues of their members, but they must also broaden their conception of service to their membership. "Unions will also be out of business if they don't convince a skeptical public that the work they do is for the good of public education, says Shanker" (Checkley, 1996, p. 8). Currently, union field representatives are public-sector counterparts to the business agents of the Teamsters and other private sector unions. What benefits might accrue if the field representatives were curriculum specialists, for example, or skilled in the application of technology to teaching and learning? And what benefits to public education might be achieved if the field representatives saw themselves as mediators of school conflicts instead of gladiators, as is so often the case?

As teachers work towards achieving a more professional standing within our society, the union cannot remain narrowly partisan. It must be flexible and inclusive, rather than exclusive. The industrial union model does not support the professional work roles sought by teacher leaders and others. As Amy Gutman (1987) noted:

If the democratic ideal of professionalism suggests that school boards and principals treat teachers as partners in determining school policy, then it also suggests that unions demand fewer fixed policies regarding curriculum, discipline, and work schedules, and more participatory structures within which teachers can join administrators and members of school boards in shaping these policies. (pp. 83–84)

The call for reform of teachers' unions has centered around several concepts. Shedd and Bacharach (1991) have envisioned a less adversarial union: one concerned less with preserving its own power. This new union would assume responsibility for the quality and quantity of its members' efforts. "Rather than negotiating rules that restrict flexibility, [the union] will look for ways to relax restrictions on both teachers and administrators" (p. 168). Johnson (1990) joins Shedd and Bacharach in recommending that the reliance on seniority in school assignments be relaxed to allow for a better fit of faculty members in the culture and direction of a school. Teacher unions must, like school districts, decentralize to allow restructured schools to shape their practice through variation and adaptation.

The Chicago Teachers Union has begun the process of moving into a more professional arena with the establishment, in 1992, of its Quest Center funded with a John D. and Katherine T. MacArthur Foundation grant of $1.1 million. The Center's major purpose is to act as a catalyst for restructuring teaching and learning. In 1993, it worked with the Chicago Board of Education on a joint project to establish a set of citywide standards for educating students. The union, through its Center, has taken "its share of risks in venturing beyond its traditional concerns over salaries, benefits, and working conditions" (Bradley, 1994, p. 34).

The joint development and implementation of educational standards clearly is a move towards establishing a more professional union that has concerns for more than job security. The concern for the profession is a positive move. However, it should be noted that this undertaking was carried out by a unit different from the regular union bureaucratic structure. This separate structure helps to keep the bread-and-butter issues separate from professional activities, a topic we will take up next.

A question to pursue in the future is whether the Quest Center will be institutionalized once the grant funding runs out.

In order to achieve the reform agenda of professionalism and restructuring, union reconceptualization of its function is not enough. The practice and structure of collective bargaining as conducted by unions and management must also change. This change can involve the elimination of collective bargaining, the transformation of collective bargaining, or the erection of a parallel process to it.

It is not likely that collective bargaining will be eliminated. It is now institutionalized in most states, and it continues to meet many of the legitimate needs of teachers. Indeed, recent legislation in this area has tended to strengthen, not weaken, collective bargaining in public education. The struggle for higher wages, better benefits, and job security are some of the areas in which unions have been most successful. The first option, elimination, will not work.

The second option—transformation—is not likely either. As McDonnell and Pascal (1988) have found, unions must continue to secure the legitimate bread-and-butter issues for their membership. Any movement toward transforming collective bargaining that in any way implicates or diminishes the securing of those benefits will probably meet with stiff resistance from teachers. While keeping the bread-and-butter issues of bargaining basically untouched, it is possible to transform teacher unions as a model of industrial unionism to a new model of professional unionism. It is not only possible, it is probably imperative. Since unions play a legitimate, legal, and a real role in the governance of schools, scrapping them is not the answer, but transforming them, while concomitantly transforming education as a whole, holds great promise.

A new relationship between school organizations and unions must be developed. The current industrial union model is not likely to aid school reform. A new model is needed that allows for professionalism and the pursuit of teacher self-interest. "Union membership," Chester Finn (1991) writes, "isn't inherently incompatible with professional behavior and good education in other countries whose schools we admire and whose teachers are at least as fully unionized as ours" (p. 91).

Koppich and Kerchner (1993) recently used the phrase *professional unionism* to describe the new teacher associations. We will use their phrase as an umbrella for the new union. According to Streshly and DeMitchell (1994), this new association will probably include some, or most, of the following elements:

- ''Rather than being adversarial and concerned with preserving their own power, the new unions will be cooperative and nonconfrontational'' (Shedd & Bacharach, 1991, p. 168). The institutionalized confrontation, or negotiated conflict, between the union and management will cease. ''Collaboration for the union does not mean co-optation or capitulation. The union maintains its organizational identity. But it is able to make its points, assert itself, and gain a professional advantage for its members in ways other than ritual saber rattling or actual concerted action'' (Koppich, 1993b, p. 7). This does not mean that all conflict will stop. There will still be conflicts that arise, which is natural, but there will not be this sustained, automatic hostility toward each other. Antipathy must give way to understanding and allow for reasonable people to disagree. Cooperation can no longer be considered a lull in the permanence of conflict.
- Related to this is union and management's propensity to ''engage in a rhetoric of mutual deprecation'' (Kerchner & Caufman, 1993, p. 15). The calculated destruction of individuals by both sides does not help education or the profession. As both sides commence bashing each other, typically around the start of negotiations, the public is left with the clear impression that the inept are leading the ill-intentioned and callous. The educators within the schools also come to believe the rhetoric. Confidence is destroyed both inside the and outside the schoolhouse gate. Improvement of education becomes doubly hard. ''Moving from a unionism built around diffidence and antagonism to one built around cooperation requires mutual respect; the vehicle for antagonism must be converted into a vehicle for getting things done'' (Kerchner & Caufman, 1993, p. 16). Koppich (1993a) suggests that the bickering remain in-house and that, when problems are aired in public, both union and management go to great lengths to cast the issue as one of differences of principled positions, not differences of personalities.
- Unions must balance the public good with teacher self-interests. In order to operate in the public domain and secure the support of the public, unions must recognize that they have public, as well as private, responsibilities. Unions cannot afford the

characterization that political scientist Norton Long made of the Chicago Teachers Union in the 1960s and 1970s. He characterized the union as "legitimating a degree of callous selfishness that surpassed that of the managerial elite of reform [government] and even the rapacity of the [Chicago political] machine" (Ayers, 1993, p. 179). The union's concept of customer must broaden. If unions want a larger voice in the public's business, it must be accountable to the public in some fashion. It is impossible to be considered a professional and not have a concomitant commitment to the public good. The union and its members must engage in serious discussion about the ways in which their professional actions impact their public responsibilities.

- The knee-jerk protection of incompetent teachers must be rethought. The union must not only speak for teachers, but it must also speak for teaching (Koppich, 1993a; Shedd & Bacharach, 1991). The union must become organizationally responsive to quality teaching. This does not mean that the union must give up its traditional stand of protecting due process rights of teachers, but due process would not be its only concern. What is good teaching, how we measure it, how we achieve it, and how we retain it should be ongoing important union topics of discussion and debate.
- One of the tenets of the industrial union is the uniform application and applicability of the negotiated contract to all sites and all employees. Reform of education and responsiveness to the customer calls for flexibility due to the differing context of different school communities. Just as decision making and governance functions are being decentralized in order to empower those individuals closest to the point of decision implementation, so must contracts have some degree of decentralization. This requires that the district office management trust that the principals will not sell out the interests of the district. Likewise, union leadership must trust that the teachers at the site will not devalue or debase the union's goals. But some form of decentralization is needed for both reform and professionalism. Teachers need to move into new leadership roles, and principals need to accommodate this

community of leaders; this cannot easily occur within the confines of standardized, centralized work rules.
* A professional union will need an attitudinal change, as well as a structural change. Similarly, management will need a change in attitude in order to accommodate the new union professionalism.

This leaves the third alternative, the construction of a new process that does not threaten the bread-and-butter achieving capacity of collective bargaining but allows for an expanded and more complex view of working conditions in education. This parallel process has been used by some Education Policy Trust Agreements (Kerchner & Mitchell, 1988; Mitchell, 1986; Koppich & Kerchner, 1988). "Where collective bargaining dealt with the 'bread-and-butter' terms and conditions of employment, trust agreements would revolve around professional problems of schools as organizations—problems of student achievement, school restructuring, staff and career development, and teacher evaluation" (Koppich & Kerchner, 1988, p. 24).

But what is an educational policy trust agreement? Kerchner and Mitchell (1988) have suggested the following content and function for this new process:

* Educational—Trust agreements are intended to deal with a broad range of educational matters: What are student achievement goals? What freedoms and what flexibility should teachers expect? What level of care and dedication should schools and the students expect?
* Policy—The new agreements are intended to move well beyond work rules and terms of employment. As we have repeatedly argued, professional teachers must deal with school policy matters. They must help to shape the general goals and overall intent of the school, not just propose formal work rules.
* Trust—These agreements are trust agreements in both common senses of the term. Formally they are related to the trust instruments used to control the use of property. Organizationally they involve each side's holding "in trust" the judgements, desires, and wishes of the other.
* Agreement—The set of educational policies that constitute the trust are explicitly negotiated agreements between organized teachers and school management, similar in this way to labor contracts. The agreements would have legal standing and could

be adjudicated either through court review or through procedures developed by the parties. (pp. 247–248)

This new type of agreement brings some important changes to the way labor relations works in schools. It is assumed that the beneficiaries of the trust agreement are the students and community, not the teachers or the school district. This is a distinct difference from collective bargaining agreements. Thus, any remedies that are fashioned because one party is not living up to the agreement is aimed at fixing the program and making progress toward the achievement of the agreement's goals and not indemnifying the staff. Another important change is the need for trust between parties. Whereas the collective bargaining process is often used when there is an absence of trust, policy agreements absolutely depend on a high degree of trust. Another change is that the policy trust agreements are finite in nature: they exist for a designated time period. Collective bargaining agreements are usually considered as remaining in full force and effect, even after its expiration, until a successor agreement is agreed upon.

An example of educational policy trust agreements is found in California, where the Stuart Foundation of San Francisco funded a one-year project in which the California Federation of Teachers and the California School Boards Association jointly selected six districts to pilot the concept. The topics for the agreements included the development of a peer assistance and review program for new teachers and for experienced teachers who are at risk, an elementary school faculty developing an interdisciplinary literature-based reading program, a performance evaluation system, and a staff development system (Koppich & Kerchner, 1988). These areas are indicative of the second wave of reform—professionalism and restructuring.

Unions and collective bargaining as potential elements of legalism where means become ends is a continuing challenge. The overreach of these activities must be kept in check. Both are part of the legalization of our schools, but neither need be allowed to descend into legalism through action, inaction, or indifference. Teachers unions, or any union in education for that matter, that maintain a purely industrial union posture will be obstacles to reform. Collective bargaining by itself is not up to the challenges proposed by systemic reform; it too must undergo reform. Unions and collective bargaining are currently inadequate for the job at hand. New processes and new attitudes must be found. Without changes in unionism and bargaining, educational reform will just be pouring old wine into new bottles

REFERENCES

Ayers, W. 1993. Chicago: A restless sea of social forces. In C. T. Kerchner and J. E. Koppich (Eds.). *A union of professionals: Labor relations and educational reform.* New York: Teachers College Press.

Bradley, A. June 22, 1994. A quest for change: The Chicago Teachers Union has emerged as an unlikely advocate of school reform. *Education Week,* pp. 34–35.

Bradley, A. May 3, 1995. Toledo Union eliminates peer-review program. *Education Week,* p. 3.

Canallos, P. S. and Walker, A. September 4, 1993. School board, teachers ok pay, reforms. *Boston Globe,* pp. 1,6.

Checkley, K. 1996. The new union: Helping teachers take a lead in education reform. *Education Update* 38(5):1, 3–5, 8.

Cresswell, A. M. and Murphy, M. J. with Kerchner, C. T. 1980. *Teachers, unions, and collective bargaining in public education.* Berkeley, CA: McCutchan Publishing Company.

DeMitchell, T. A. 1993. Collective bargaining, professionalism, and restructuring, *International Journal of Educational Reform* 2:77-81.

DeMitchell, T. A. and Barton, R. W. 1994. Collective bargaining: Barrier or vehicle for school reform. Paper Presentation, *New England Educational Research Organization Annual Convention,* Rockport, Maine.

Finn, Jr., C. E. 1991. *We must take charge: Our schools and our future.* New York: The Free Press.

Fossey, R. and Miles, K. 1991. *School-based management in the Boston Public Schools: Why isn't it working?* Unpublished report to the Mayor of Boston.

Glaser, J. 1989. Alternative labor relations practices: A second look. *Thrust for Educational Leadership* 18:32–37.

Gutman, A. 1987. *Democratic education.* Princeton, New Jersey: Princeton University Press.

Johnson, S. M. 1987. "Can schools be reformed at the bargaining table?" *Teachers College Record* 89(2):269–280.

Johnson, S. M. 1990. *Teachers at work: Achieving success in our schools.* New York: Basic Books, Inc. Publishers.

Kerchner, C. T. and Caufman, K. D. 1993. Building the airplane while it is rolling down the runway. In *A union of professionals: Labor relations and educational reform,* edited by C. T. Kerchner and J. E. Koppich, pp. 1–24. New York: Teachers College Press.

Kerchner, C. T. and Mitchell, D. E. 1988. *The changing idea of a teachers' union.* New York: The Falmer Press.

Koppich, J. E. 1993a. "Getting started: A primer on professional unionism," in *A union of professionals: Labor relations and educational reform.* C. T. Kerchner and J. E. Koppich, Eds., New York: Teachers College Press.

Koppich, J. E. 1993b. "How professional unionism challenges public bureaucracy," paper presented at the American Educational Research Association Annual Convention, Atlanta, Georgia.

Koppich, J. E. and Kerchner, C. T. 1993. "Negotiating reform: Preliminary findings," In S. C. Jacobson and R. Berne (Eds.). *Reforming education: The emerging systemic approach.* Thousand Oaks, CA: Corwin Press, Inc.

Koppich, J. E. and Kerchner, C. T. September 1988. The trust agreement project: Broadening the vision of school labor-management relations—A first-year progress report, Policy Paper No. PP88-9-7. Berkeley, CA: Policy Analysis for California Education.

Lieberman, M. Winter 1984. "Educational reform and teacher bargaining," *Government Union Review* 5(1):54−75.

McDonnell, L. M. and Pascal, A. April 1988. *Teacher unions and educational reform.* Santa Monica, CA: Rand.

Mitchell, D. 1986. "Policy trust agreements: A better approach to school labor relations," *Thrust for Educational Leadership* 18(9):8−12.

Shedd, J. B. and Bacharach, S. B. 1991. *Tangled hierarchies: Teachers as professionals and the management of schools.* San Francisco: Jossey-Bass Publishers.

Streshly, W. A. and DeMitchell, T. A. 1994. *Teacher unions and TQE: Building quality labor relations.* Thousand Oaks, CA: Corwin Press, Inc.

Toch, T. 1991. *In the name of excellence: The struggle to reform the nation's schools, why it's failing, and what should be done.* New York: Oxford University Press.

Wise, A. E. 1979. *Legislated learning: The Bureaucratization of the American classroom.* Berkeley, CA: University of California Press.

CHAPTER 3

Site-Based Management in a Collective Bargaining Environment: Can We Mix Oil and Water?

> *Don't think that, by itself, [school-based management] will produce anything.*
>
> — Albert Shanker, AFT president
> (Wen & Snyder, 1988)
>
> *The school-based management that has been heralded in this town is bogus.*
>
> — High school headmaster
> Boston Public Schools, 1991
>
> *We shall never learn to . . . respect our real calling . . . , unless we have taught ourselves to consider everything as moonshine, compared with the education of the heart.*
>
> — Sir Walter Scott

Site-based management, with its promise of teacher empowerment, shared decision making, and collegial relations between teachers and administrators, has become a popular school reform strategy. Indeed, several state legislatures now require school districts to implement site-based management based on the belief that this is a promising means of improving the quality of the schools.

Frequently, site-based management advocates discuss the merits of this reform strategy without reference to collective bargaining. Yet, when site-based management and collective bargaining are examined together, it is clear that a fundamental conflict exists between the two concepts. Site-based management, with its emphasis on collaboration and cooperation among educators, is wholly inconsistent with the adversarial nature of collective bargaining that exists in many schools.

This chapter identifies the ways in which site-based management and collective bargaining are in conflict and examines how this conflict can hinder the effective implementation of site-based management. With forethought, some of these conflicts can be minimized or reconciled, and this chapter suggests some ways this can be done. Ultimately, however, the climate of antagonism that accompanies collective bargaining in many school districts, particularly urban districts, will not be changed by the mere introduction of a novel school reform strategy.

SITE-BASED MANAGEMENT AND PUBLIC-SECTOR COLLECTIVE BARGAINING: PHILOSOPHIES IN CONFLICT

In many ways, introducing site-based management in a collective bargaining environment is like trying to mix oil and water. The two concepts are fundamentally at odds. First, collective bargaining is adversarial, while site-based management nurtures collegiality. Second, collective bargaining assumes that teachers have no responsibility for determining education policy, while site-based management encourages teacher participation in educational policy decisions. Third, collective bargaining strives for uniform working conditions for teachers, while site-based management permits diversity from school site to school site.

Collective bargaining is adversarial, while site-based management is collegial.

In 1935, Congress passed the National Labor Relations Act (NLRA), the nation's first modern labor law, to restrain the violent confrontations between large corporations and their industrial workers that were common during the Great Depression. Indeed, the United States Supreme Court has referred to the NLRA as a substitute for "economic warfare." Since that time, industrial labor relations in the United States have been based on the premise that workers and employers are adversaries.

Collective bargaining in public education did not begin in earnest until the 1960s, but the structure of labor relations that developed in the schools is virtually identical to the industrial model laid out by the NLRA. Like its private sector counterpart, collective bargaining in the public schools is based on the premise that teachers and school boards have fundamentally different interests.

Labor relations in the schools have never fallen to the level of violent confrontation that is the heritage of industrial labor relations, but in urban districts, hostility between unionized teachers and school boards is often evident, particularly during impasses in contract negotiations. As two commentators wrote, it is the appearance of "unvarnished self-interest," often evident during money disputes, that has made it difficult for the public to accept teaching as a "moral occupation" (Kerchner & Mitchell, 1988, p. 240).

One of the great attractions of site-based management has been its potential for introducing collegiality and cooperation into the relationship between teachers and school boards, qualities that often seem incompatible with the collective bargaining relationship. When the Boston School Committee negotiated a site-based management provision into its collective bargaining agreement with the Boston Teachers Union, the *Boston Globe* hailed the new contract as the beginning of a new era in labor relations in the strife-torn Boston school system. "The new agreement," the *Globe* editorialized, "proves that teachers and city officials can become partners rather than adversaries in an important venture—the task of educating children" (Editorial, Partners in Education, 1990).

Unfortunately, the reality has been far different from the expectation. There is almost no evidence that site-based management has changed the culture of conflict that exists in most urban school districts. An independent analysis on site-based management, prepared for the Los Angeles Unified School District after the first year that the program was in place, found that the "institutional antagonism" between management and labor undermined the effectiveness of site-based management in the nation's second largest school district (Wilson, 1992, pp. 42–43). A study of the grievances filed by Boston teachers before and after the introduction of site-based management in the Boston schools found that the pattern of adversarial problem solving had continued almost without change (Fossey & Miles, 1991).

Collective bargaining assumes clear distinctions between the responsibilities of management and labor. Site-based management assumes shared decision making and teacher participation in educational policy decisions.

In the private sector, collective bargaining assumes a clear distinction between the role of management and labor in the work place. Labor has the right to bargain with management about wages and working conditions, but the employer is not required to bargain with workers about matters that are within the "core of entrepreneurial control" (*Fibreboard Paper Products v. NLRB,* 1964). Those decisions are the prerogative of management. In the public sector, school districts are also required to bargain with teachers about wages and working conditions, but districts are not obliged to bargain about matters of educational policy.

In practice, of course, the difference between working conditions and educational policy is often hard to discern, and the state courts have rendered many opinions trying to distinguish between the two. Nevertheless, the principle has remained more or less intact that teachers' unions cannot force school committees to bargain over matters of educational policy.

Site-based management runs counter to the collective bargaining model of distinct realms for management and labor. Site-based management encourages teachers to assume responsibility for designing education programs and perhaps for participating in hiring decisions and budget preparation. More importantly, site-based management generally assumes that teachers will share accountability for student performance. Indeed, site-based management tends to reverse the realms of management and labor with regard to policymaking responsibilities, drawing policymaking authority away from the school board and the central administration office and lodging it among teachers, principals, and sometimes parents.

Collective bargaining strives for uniformity in the interest of fairness. Site-based management strives for diversity in the interest of creativity.

One of the important protections collective bargaining offers workers is the assurance that workers will be treated uniformly with regard to wages and working conditions. In the public sector, teachers' unions insist on a uniform salary scale, and they have resisted merit pay plans that could allow school officials to pay individual teachers at different rates. Teachers' unions have also resisted policies that give administrators unlimited discretion to assign teachers to vacant positions. The unions prefer assignment and transfer plans to be based on objective criteria, like seniority.

In contrast, site-based management encourages diversity at the school level. Individual schools are not bound by bureaucratic policies imposed by central office administrators or by union work rules. Instead, the staff at each school site is free to develop creative solutions to the educational problems they confront. This philosophy may give teachers and site administrators more control over their work lives, but it also means that teachers' working conditions may vary from school site to school site. Thus, the uniformity of a districtwide contract would have to give way to balkanization by site-based needs.

COMMON PROBLEMS WITH INTEGRATING SITE-BASED MANAGEMENT INTO A COLLECTIVE BARGAINING ENVIRONMENT

Given the conflict between the philosophies of collective bargaining and site-based management, it is not surprising that problems arise when site-based management is introduced in the collective-bargaining environment that exists in most urban schools. Following are some of the problems that school districts face.

The adversarial grievance process counteracts efforts to engage in collegial problem solving and shared decision making.

School districts and teachers' unions often agree to insert site-based management provisions into the bodies of otherwise standard union contracts. These contracts almost always contain grievance procedures that authorize union members to file grievances about contract violations. Unfortunately, even after site-based management is adopted, the parties often revert to their adversarial grievance procedure to settle their disputes.

Grievances usually proceed in three steps. At the first step, a principal hears the grievance and decides whether to deny it or grant a remedy. If the grievance is denied, the union can appeal to a senior-level administrator. If the administrator denies relief, the dispute generally goes to an arbitrator, who is usually given the authority to make a binding decision. Often, the arbitrator is a labor lawyer with little or no expertise in pedagogy or educational policy (Finch & Nagel, 1984). As a result, arbitrators frequently issue binding decisions based solely on labor law principles but which have serious consequences for a school district's educational program.

For example, in 1990, after site-based management had been adopted in the Boston schools, the teachers union and the school committee argued over whether special education teachers were required under the union contract to fill out a new form designed to document the effectiveness of special education services. An arbitrator ruled that the teachers should not have been required to use the new forms until the matter had been submitted to collective bargaining. Based on the testimony that the new forms required an extra five minutes a day to complete, or a total of two hours per teacher over the course of one school year, the arbitrator awarded every teacher who filled out the new forms to be paid for two hours' work (Boston Teachers Union and Boston School Committee, 1990).

It is difficult to see how site-based management is going to foster accountability and shared decision making if teachers and administrators are unable to agree on the best way to document the effectiveness of special education services without resorting to an arbitrator. It is also difficult to see how educators will be able to teach problem-solving skills to children, if they do not have those skills themselves.

In this regard, Dade County Public Schools and the United Teachers of Dade took a step in the right direction when they created a special grievance procedure for schools participating in site-based management and shared decision making. Under that procedure, teacher grievances that are not resolved at the site level are appealed to a grievance committee made up of administrators and union representatives. If the dispute is not resolved at that level, the matter can be appealed by the union to a joint hearing body made up of the school superintendent and the union vice president. Only after two attempts at joint problem solving does the dispute go to binding arbitration.

Site-based management decisions conflict with the union contracts of nonteaching employees.

Too often, school districts institute site-based management as if the only employees' group that needs to be consulted is the teachers' union. In fact, most urban school districts have relationships with several unions, and the work rules imposed by the union contracts of nonteaching employees can be a major impediment to site-based management.

A Boston principal described a typical example of the way union work rules for nonteaching employees can hamper the goals of a school-site council:

> The major cost of our after school program was paying for custodial overtime because you can't have a building in Boston open after hours unless you pay custodians time and a half. The custodian in this building is getting paid more than the teachers who are running the program! We petitioned for a waiver — in an SBM school you can do that. Then we were told that's part of the custodial contract. I said, "Look. I'm in the building anyway for the program. I'm here 'till five thirty. I know how to open the building, lock the building, set the alarm; I know how to turn on and off the electricity and all that — I'm the principal! I'm here so why can't I?" "No, no, that's the custodial contract; they'll grieve it if you violate the contract," etc. So we couldn't do that. (Wilson, 1990, pp. 54–55)

A related problem arises when a school district, acting in concert with the teachers' union, implements site-based management without involving the nonunion employees whose support is necessary for the innovation to succeed. That happened in Rochester, New York, where Rochester principals sued to enjoin the implementation of a peer assistance review program, arguing that the procedures agreed to between the school board and the teachers' union infringed on the statutory authority of the principals (Johnson, 1990). That dispute was ultimately resolved, and the new program was instituted with the principals' involvement, but the principals' support had been missing at a critical time because they had not been included in the negotiations process.

Involving every collective bargaining unit in the site-based planning process will be difficult, and the larger the district, the more difficult the process will be. [New York City, the nation's largest district, has contractual relations with thirty-nine unions (Mann, 1984).] It may not be easy to persuade bus drivers, secretaries, custodians, lunch aides, and bus monitors that their work rules should be adjusted to permit a particular site council's innovation to be introduced. Nevertheless, if these unions are ignored when site-based management is introduced, then this reform effort will be relegated to the periphery of school operations or doomed to failure.

School sites cannot make staffing decisions because of seniority-

based transfer rules contained in the collective bargaining contract.

Educators debate whether site-based management should delegate budget-making authority to individual schools, but most would agree that site-based management cannot be successful unless the professional staff members at a school have a voice in staffing decisions. But in many districts, seniority-based transfer rules in union contracts require districts to give vacant positions to the senior teacher who applies. In these districts, site-based planning councils have no way of building a team of educators that share a common philosophy or have the necessary mix of skills.

Site-based management, even when negotiated into the union contract, does not change the adversarial nature of school culture at the site level. Tensions reemerge when it comes time to negotiate a new union contract.

School districts and teachers unions generally agree to implement site-based management as a part of a contract settlement. Teachers usually receive significant pay raises for agreeing to participate in site-based management, raises that reflect the fact that teachers have agreed to accept more responsibility for educational programs and to be accountable for results.

Unfortunately, the implementation of site-based management and the salary increases that go with it often fail to change the climate of conflict that pervades labor relations in urban schools. This climate of conflict reappears at the next contract negotiations, when teachers may engage in job actions from "working to rule" (refusing to perform tasks not specifically required by contract) to engaging in strikes.

Newton Public Schools, for example, an affluent suburb west of Boston, is a site-based management school district. That fact did not prevent teachers from working to rule during contract negotiations in 1992, a practice that prevented teachers from meeting with parents after school hours or even, in some instances, writing letters of reference for college-bound high school students (Newton teachers, 1992). Similarly, in Rochester, New York, another district that embraced site-based management, some teachers boycotted site-based planning meetings during difficult contract negotiations a few years ago.

Site-based management is introduced without instituting other reforms, such as improving the recruiting process.

In the final analysis, no school reform model will succeed unless a school district hires and retains top-quality teachers. Any plan to implement school-based management must be accompanied by professional recruiting practices.

In *Who Will Teach? Policies That Matter,* Richard Murnane and colleagues (1991) discussed the wide variation in the quality of school districts' recruiting practices. They found that the districts that were the most successful in recruiting top-quality teachers were the ones that were able to offer jobs to attractive candidates early in the recruiting season and to specify the school where the teacher would work and the specific grade and subjects that the new hire would teach.

Who Will Teach? points out that school districts with poor recruiting practices are sometimes hampered by seniority-based transfer rules that create delays in identifying the locations where vacancies exist. As discussed above, these are the same rules that can prevent principals and teachers from selecting the teachers who will join their staffs. Although these rules were negotiated into union contracts for a good reason, to ensure all teachers fair access to the most desirable teaching jobs, where they are enforced inflexibly, they can cause districts to lose the best job applicants to districts that can identify vacancies sooner and make faster and more specific job offers.

Changes in union transfer rules cannot be unilaterally abolished by a school board. They must be changed during good-faith bargaining between the school board and the teachers' union. Probably the best time to accomplish this is during the negotiations that introduce site-based management into the union contract.

CONCLUSIONS AND RECOMMENDATIONS

If school districts introduce school-based management in an adversarial collective bargaining environment without examining the entire relationship between the district and its unions, school-based management will achieve nothing. Thus, before adopting school-based management, they should consider the following recommendations:

- The essential terms of school-based management must become a part of the collective bargaining agreement and not simply a unilateral policy of the school board. To be successful, school-based management must become a binding contractual commitment between teachers and school boards.

- If state law permits, the adversarial grievance process should be amended to require teachers and administrators to share the responsibility for solving education problems and implementing solutions. Problems should not be delegated to a noneducator for a decision.
- The terms of classified employees union contracts should be reviewed to determine whether these contracts interfere with the successful implementation of school-based management. If so, the school board must make an effort to amend these agreements through the collective bargaining process.
- Principals and site-based planning councils should have a role in hiring and transfer decisions that affect their school. This may involve changing the seniority-based transfer rules that are commonly part of union contracts.
- School-based management should be accompanied by professional recruiting efforts to insure quality personnel in the schools. Union rules that hinder the recruiting process should be changed or eliminated.
- Before agreeing to implement school-based planning, school boards should try to get a commitment from the teachers union that teachers will not boycott site-based management activities as part of a work slowdown or work-to-rule action.

All these recommendations will help make school-based management successful in a collective bargaining environment, but it is doubtful whether an urban school district will be able to implement them all. Classified employees may not see it in their interest to amend union work rules to aid site-based management. Custodians, for example, may not want to give up work rules that guarantee them overtime pay, even if doing so benefits a school site's educational program. Some state laws mandate grievance procedures that end in binding arbitration, prohibiting districts and unions from changing the way they resolve disputes, even if they agree to do so.

In the final analysis, school-based management will not be successful unless the culture of confrontation and hostility that exists in many school districts is changed by a genuine understanding that the learning environment requires a collegial relationship among educators. Such a change will require something more than adoption of site-based management. It will require all the parties to collective bargaining to pursue their individual interests in such a way that collegiality is not damaged or destroyed. Such a change will require "education of the heart."

REFERENCES

Boston Teachers Union and Boston School Committee. (1990). American Arbitration Association Case No. 1139-0518-90.

Editorial. Partners in education. (1990, January 24). *Boston Globe.*

Fibreboard Paper Products v. NLRB, 379 U.S. 203, 223, 85 S.Ct. 398, 409 (1964) (Stewart, J., concurring).

Finch, M. and Nagel, T. W. (1984). Collective bargaining in the public schools. *Wisconsin Law Review* 1984:1573–1670.

Fossey, R. and Miles, K. (1991). School-based management in the Boston public schools: Why isn't it working? Unpublished report.

Johnson, S. M. (1990). Teachers, power, and school change. In W. H. Clune and J. F. Witle (Eds.), *Choice and control in American education. Vol. 2: The practice of choice, decentralization and restructuring.* London: Falmer Press.

Kerchner, C. T. and Mitchell, D. E. (1988). *The changing idea of a teachers' union.* London: Falmer.

Mann, D. (1984). Education in New York City: Public schools for whom? In G. Grace (Ed.), *Education and the city.* London: Routledge & Kegan Paul.

Murnane, R., Singer, J. D., Willett, J. B., Kemple, J. J., and Olsen, R. J. (1991). *Who will teach? Policies that matter.* Cambridge, Massachusetts: Harvard University Press.

Newton teachers say no extras. (1992, December 3). *Boston Globe.*

Wen, P. and Snyder, S. (1988, November 1). Sweeping changes in schools urged. *Boston Globe*, p. 1.

Wilson, S. F. (1992). *Reinventing the schools, a radical plan for Boston.* Boston: Pioneer Institute for Public Policy Research.

PART TWO

ACCOUNTABILITY MECHANISM: INSIDE AND OUTSIDE THE CLASSROOM

CHAPTER 4

Who Decides Who Will Teach Our Children – The Community or the Profession?

If education is a social enterprise, then the civilization of the future will bear a close resemblance to the teachers of the present.

—Joseph C. McElhannon
"The Social Failure of the Teacher" (1929)

Respectable citizens indulge privately in conduct they forbid teachers.

—Howard K. Beale
Are American Teachers Free? An Analysis of Restraints upon the Freedom of Teaching in American Schools (1936)

"Who shall teach our children?" is one of the great recurring questions in the history of education. From the trial of Socrates for corrupting the youth of ancient Athens to the contemporary school reform debate, parents and community leaders have always been concerned about the intellectual and moral quality of teachers.

In the United States, concerns about teachers' deportment date from at least the beginning of the "one best system." Willard Elsbree, in 1939, noted that the conduct of American school teachers has always been a matter of public interest.

The centrality of teachers to our system of education can hardly be overstated. As discussed in the first chapter, the bureaucratic reform efforts of the first wave that did not focus on improving the conditions for learning and teaching or on professionalizing teaching were doomed to failure or, worse, to become mere window dressing. The second

51

reform wave tried to correct this oversight. A cornerstone of the second wave was the drive to professionalize teaching.

The Education Commission of the States (Green, 1986) noted that "making teaching a profession means augmenting teachers' rights and responsibilities" (p. 7). This begs the question of who should determine the extent and context of responsibility. Chapter 5 will look at this issue of responsibility (or accountability), with a lens focused on classroom teaching. More specifically, that chapter will revisit educational malpractice in light of new research on best practices and the movement towards national standards for curriculum and national teacher certification. This chapter reviews the issue of accountability from a different perspective—the personal out-of-school behavior of educators as an indicator of fitness to teach.

Since teachers are central to education, reform that does not take into account who is in front of the class may miss the point of real reform. There is no magic in programs; there is only magic in people. Therefore, those persons who have the authority to decide who can teach our children are, in many ways, the gatekeepers for education. The question to be explored in this chapter is where that authority should reside—the community or the profession. This chapter will examine the issue of the private lives of teachers as a factor in deciding who shall teach our children. It asks to whom is the teacher accountable, but also what morals should guide a teacher's actions both in the classroom and outside the schoolhouse gate.

Traditionally, educators have been compelled to adhere more strictly to the community's moral codes than most other professions or occupations. Teachers have been considered holders of a special position of trust and responsibility because of their relationship with the community's children. "The courts have interpreted this concept by attaching the status of exemplar to the profession of teaching, thus holding teachers to a higher standard than the average citizen" (DeMitchell & De-Mitchell, 1990, p. 381). And the conduct of greatest concern was that which took place outside of the schoolhouse gate. One teacher, reflecting on this phenomenon, remarked, "How I conduct my classes seems to be of no great interest to the school authorities, but what I do when school is not in session concerns them tremendously" (Beale, 1936, p. 395).

WHO SHALL BE THE GATEKEEPER?

The history of education in the United States is replete with numerous examples of stringent ordinances and school board regulations mandating a higher standard of conduct for teachers than for other community members. Parents who smoked, drank, gambled, lied, and committed adultery demanded that a teacher's conduct be above their own. It was and still is believed that teachers must lead an exemplary life so as to properly mold children's virtues. With great sincerity, parents and the community ''believe a teacher should be a public servant who serves the community . . . and whose influence will give their children the characters they themselves aspired to and failed to attain'' (Beale, 1936, p. 407). The community has asserted at various times that married teachers should not be employed; that a teacher should not be allowed to make pacifist statements during World War II; and that wearing of transparent hosiery, low-necked dresses, cosmetics, and not fastening their galoshes all the way up was inappropriate; more recently, a teacher was dismissed for going through a divorce (DeMitchell, 1993).

The education profession, on the other hand, has asserted that teachers should have the right to a private life and that their privacy should be protected unless it can be shown that the behavior directly and negatively impacts their teaching or the efficient operation of the school. Such decisions as *Jarvella v. Willoughby-Eastlake City School District* (1967) illustrate this point. The court, in overturning Jarvella's dismissal for writing questionable letters to a former student who recently graduated from high school, wrote:

> The private conduct of a man, who is also a teacher, is a proper concern to those who employ him only to the extent it mars him as a teacher, who is also a man. Where his professional achievement is unaffected, where the school community is placed in no jeopardy, his private acts are his own business and may not be the basis of discipline. (p. 146)

Thus, the private acts of a teacher were considered just that, private, unless it could be shown that those acts damaged his or her ability to perform the job.

The tension between the community and the profession over control of who decides who shall teach our children is as strong today as it was in earlier times. Both the community and the profession try to assert their role as gatekeeper. One need look no further than the issue of gay or lesbian teachers in the classroom to gauge the virulence of this issue.

COMMUNITY CONTROL—EXEMPLAR

The system of schooling in the early days of the Republic was predominantly rural and clearly controlled by the community, with some exceptions in the urban centers of the east. The schools were considered an extension of the local community. They were largely unbureaucratic and exhibited only rudimentary professionalism. "With no bureaucracy to serve as a buffer between himself and patrons, with little sense of being part of a professional establishment, the teacher found himself subordinated to the community" (Tyack & Hansot, 1982, p. 19). The system of boarding teachers around the district provided a mechanism for subordinating the teacher to the community, as well as monitoring the personal life of the teacher.

The community's control over teachers was pervasive. Not only was the teacher's classroom conduct and skills keenly evaluated, almost all facets of the teacher's personal life were scrutinized. As previously mentioned, because of a teacher's close relationship with children, teachers were considered mandatory role models. The generalized moral expectations of the community shaped the behavior of educators both in and outside the classroom. Tyack and Hansot (1982) note that "evidence abounds that townspeople kept a vigilant eye on the out-of-class behavior of educators, and that the moral 'lapses' resulted in firings more often than did incompetence in the classroom" (p. 174).

The control and degree of pressure that the community brought to bear on a teacher was formidable. Such activities as dancing, smoking, drinking, divorce, marriage, dating, and pregnancy were looked at askance by school authorities, and frequently, their indulgence brought about disciplinary action. The community exercised control by mandating community spirit, whereby teachers had to donate both time and money to community activities.

Joseph C. McElhannon, writing in 1929, underscored this point in his analysis of the efficiency reports of 893 teachers from 1923 to 1928. Of the 893 teachers he reviewed, 343 were not reelected. The reasons for nonreelection, among others, included: "They were not identified with the community" (191 teachers); "they were more interested in the town shieks" (126 teachers); "they frowned upon church and Sunday school" (79 teachers); "they left Friday and returned on Monday to work" (53 teachers); and "they were grossly immoral" (22 teachers). Clearly, the teacher must identify with the community. The teacher was expected to uphold and adhere to standards of thought and action. He or she was supposed to participate in all things, but to determine none. Beale (1936) wrote: "The teacher is still 'only a teacher,' not entitled to vigorous views on things that really matter in the community if his views differ from those generally accepted'' (p. 244).

Teachers led precarious professional lives. They were scrutinized in the classroom and dictated to outside it. *Horosko v. School District of Mount Pleasant Township* (1939) illustrates the breadth of control that the community had over the private lives of teachers. Horosko was a primary school teacher in the small Pennsylvania community of Mount Pleasant. She married the owner of a restaurant located 125 feet from the school where she taught. Beer was served in the restaurant and a pinball machine and a slot machine were maintained for the patrons' pleasure. Various forms of dice were also played on the premises. Horosko worked as a waitress after school hours and during the summer months. Students and citizens of the community saw her shake dice with the customers, instruct customers how to play the pinball machine, and take an occasional drink of beer.

Although there was no charge or evidence of disorderly conduct or excessive drinking, she was dismissed by the school board for immorality. She fought her dismissal all the way to the Supreme Court of Pennsylvania, which upheld her dismissal. The court discussed the exemplary status that teachers were placed in and its relationship to immorality:

> Immorality is not essentially confined to deviation from sex morality; it may be such a course of action as offends the morals of the community and is a bad example to the youth whose ideals a teacher is supposed to foster and to elevate. . . . It has always been the recognized duty of the teacher to conduct himself in such a way as to command the respect and good will of the community, though one result of the choice of a teacher's vocation may be to deprive him of the same freedom of action enjoyed by persons in other vocations. (p. 868)

The breadth of control that the community had over the private lives of its teachers was pervasive. The community decided who shall teach its children not just through the process of teacher selection, but also through who was retained.

The community's assertion of ownership, or guardian of accountability, of deciding who shall teach our children is not limited to the nineteenth and early twentieth centuries. In 1959, the Illinois Court of Appeals upheld the dismissal of a teacher who had been arrested four times for public intoxication (*Scott v. Board of Education of Alton,* 1959). In sustaining the dismissal, the appellate court held that a "teacher is . . . a leader of pupils of tender age, resulting in admiration and emulation, and that the Board might properly fear the effect of social conduct in public, not in keeping with the dignity and leadership they desired from teachers" (p. 3). A California court in 1972 (*Watson v. Board of Education*, 1972), with a similar fact pattern of public alcohol abuse, also found that teachers are regarded by the public as exemplars.

The concept of teacher as community role model is illustrated in a 1986 case, *McBroom v. Board of Education, District No. 205* (1986), where a teacher was dismissed for the theft of a student's check. The court wrote: "We are cognizant of the special position of leadership occupied by a teacher who serves as a role model and instills the basic values of our society" (p. 869). Likewise, a Massachusetts Appeals Court (*Perryman v. School Committee of Boston*, 1983) wrote: "Teachers hold a position of special trust because 'as role models for our children they have an extensive and peculiar opportunity to impress their attitudes and views upon their pupils' "(p. 750).

The community's expectation that teachers act as exemplary role models has been consistent since the early days of our Republic. But the assertion of exemplar as an accountability mechanism would be contested in the latter half of the twentieth century.

PROFESSIONAL AUTONOMY – NEXUS

As discussed previously, the schools of the nineteenth century were controlled by the local community. School reformers in the middle of that century worked at transforming those schools. David Tyack's (1974) important work, *The One-Best System,* traced the consolidation and transformation of the common school. Our interest in this history is the rise of the profession as a counterbalance to the control of the community. Tyack noted this process when he wrote:

> This movement to take control of the rural common school away from the local community and to turn it over to the professionals was part of a more general organizational revolution in American education in which laymen lost much of their direct control over the schools. (p. 25)

The professionals expanded their influence over the schools, establishing school systems and bureaucratizing those systems. But it would take a force outside the schools to give them a voice to assert a theory of accountability different from exemplar over the issue of the role of the private lives of teachers.

The acceleration of individual rights in the 1960s and 1970s caught teachers in its whirlwind. There was a swing toward greater freedom of action and speech. Individual rights were now being balanced against community interests.

Probably the case that best illustrates the move away from the community's ability to police the private lives of teachers is *Morrison v. State Board of Education* (1969) (DeMitchell, 1993).

Marc S. Morrison was a successful teacher in the Lowell Joint School District for a number of years prior to 1964. A review of his record revealed no complaints or criticism of his performance as a teacher.

In 1963, he developed a close friendship with Mr. and Mrs. Schneringer; Mr. Schneringer taught in the same school district as Morrison. When the Schneringer's experienced marital difficulties, Morrison gave counsel and advice to Mr. Schneringer, who visited Morrison's apartment frequently. During a one-week period in April of 1963, the two men engaged in a limited, noncriminal physical relationship on four separate occasions in Morrison's apartment. Morrison described these activities as being homosexual in nature. Morrison was never accused or convicted of any criminal activity, nor was there any evidence of continued homosexual activity by Morrison after the incidents.

One year after the April incidents, Schneringer reported the homosexual conduct with Morrison to the superintendent of the district. Morrison resigned his teaching position in May of 1964. Nineteen months after the report was made, the State Board of Education of California conducted a hearing concerning the possible revocation of Morrison's life teaching credential. No evidence was presented at the hearing that Morrison had ever committed any act of misconduct while teaching. The board of education, nevertheless, revoked the life credential some three years after the Schneringer incidents, concluding that Morrison's behavior constituted immorality and unprofessional conduct.

Morrison sought a writ of mandamus from the Superior Court of Los Angeles to compel the board to set aside its decision and restore his credential. The court denied the writ. Morrison appealed, and the Supreme Court of California heard the case.

The California State Supreme Court's decision was seminal. The court stated: "Today's morals may be tomorrow's ancient and absurd customs" (p. 383). In pursuit of the relationship between a teacher's out-of-school activities and dismissal for immorality, the court held:

> Terms such as "immoral or unprofessional conduct" or "moral turpitude" stretch over so wide a range that they embrace an unlimited area of conduct. In using them the Legislature surely did not mean to endow the employing agency with the power to dismiss any employee whose personal, private conduct incurred its disapproval. (p. 382)

The court offered a number of considerations that would be helpful in determining the impact of a teacher's out-of-school conduct on the school setting. These include the following:

(1) Whether the conduct adversely affects the students or fellow teachers

(2) The proximity or remoteness in time of conduct

(3) The age of the students that the teacher works with

(4) The extenuating or aggravating circumstances surrounding the conduct

(5) The praiseworthiness or blameworthiness of the motives resulting in the conduct

(6) The likelihood of recurrence

(7) The extent to which disciplinary action may inflict a chilling effect on the rights of teachers

A new theory of accountability for teacher behavior was born — nexus. This theory asserts that it must be demonstrated that the teacher's behavior has adversely affected the school or reduced the teacher's effectiveness in the classroom. The profession now had a theory it could assert as it struggled to remove the weight of community control from its shoulders.

The contest between exemplar and nexus is illustrated in *Fisher v. Snyder* (1973). Prior to this case, actions on the part of a teacher that raised the mere specter of wrongdoing would negatively implicate the status of exemplar.[1]

Fisher, a middle-aged, divorced, high school teacher in a rural Nebraska community, was discharged from her position because she had overnight male guests stay in her one-bedroom apartment. Most of the guests were young men and friends of Mrs. Fisher's son who taught school in a neighboring town. The hotel accommodations were limited in the town, and upon advice of the school board's secretary, Mrs. Fisher extended the hospitality of her residence to her son's friends. There was no attempt to conceal the presence of her visitors.

In the spring of 1972, Mrs. Fisher was notified that her contract would not be renewed at the end of the school year. After exhausting her administrative remedy, she was dismissed for unbecoming conduct outside the classroom. The school board took the following position:

> The inferences from her social behavior are that there was a strong potential of sexual misconduct. The board does not actually accuse Mrs. Fisher of immoral conduct but of social misbehavior that is not conducive to the maintenance of the integrity of the public school system. (p. 377)

Mrs. Fisher turned to the federal court system. She brought an action against the board members under 42 U.S.C. 1983, alleging that her dismissal was unconstitutional. The district court held that her dismissal was impermissible because it was arbitrary and capricious. The court ordered her reinstated. The school board appealed.

The court of appeals affirmed the lower court's ruling. It based its decision on the argument that "each of the stated reasons . . . is trivial, or is unrelated to the educational process or to working relationships within the educational institution, or is wholly unsupported by a basis in fact" (p. 377).

A school board cannot infer wrongdoing; it must prove wrongdoing before a teacher can be dismissed. Just because a teacher becomes the focus of a community controversy does not automatically mean that the teacher should be dismissed without a showing of harm to the educational environment.

One year later, again in America's heartland, another nexus case was heard. Richard Erb taught art, coached wrestling, assisted with football, and acted as senior class sponsor at Nishua Valley Community School. He taught there for eleven years. Margaret Johnson taught home economics in the same school.

Mr. Johnson became suspicious about his wife, Margaret's, frequent late-night absences. One night, Mr. Johnson hid in the trunk of his wife's car. She drove the car to school that night and worked for awhile and later drove the car to a secluded area where she met Erb. Mr. Johnson, while still hiding in the trunk, witnessed his wife and Erb having sexual intercourse in the back seat of her car.

Later, Mr. Johnson complained to the school authorities, hoping to remove Erb from the school. Upon hearing of the complaint, Erb offered to resign, but the local school board would not accept his resignation. In a hearing into the matter before the State Board of Public Instruction, the local board president and several parents testified that the community had forgiven Erb and that he still maintained the respect of the community. Nevertheless, Erb's certificate was revoked by a vote of five to four. Erb sought relief from the courts.

The trial court held that Erb's adulterous conduct was a sufficient cause upon which to base the revocation of his teaching certificate. On appeal, the Iowa Supreme Court, relying heavily on Morrison, reversed the lower court's decision (*Erb v. Iowa State Board of Education of Public Instruction,* 1974). The high court held that the adulterous conduct in question must adversely affect the teacher's performance before revocation could be upheld. The supreme court concluded that there was no evidence of such adverse effect; a nexus was not established between the personal conduct of the teacher and a corresponding detriment to the school or the teacher's ability to teach.

WHO SHALL DECIDE?

Two major parties have vied for the role of the gatekeeper, who lets those individuals into the classroom who have passed their particular accountability test — exemplar or nexus. The first party, the community, asserts the theory of exemplar. "The school teacher has traditionally been regarded as a moral example for the students" (*Board of Education of Hopkins County v. Wood,* 1986, p. 839). While the dominant view historically, the concept of exemplar is still vibrant and very much alive today. In 1981, the court in *Chicago Board of Education v. Payne* (1981) stated: "We are aware of the special position occupied by a teacher in our society. As a consequence of that elevated stature, a teacher's actions are subject to much greater scrutiny than that given to the activities of the average person" (p. 748).

The second party to the contested ownership of the gate is the profession, including unions and professional associations. The theory advanced by the profession is nexus. M. Chester Nolte, noted school law commentator, has described nexus thus: "A school employee cannot be penalized for misbehavior unless a school board can prove that such misbehavior diminishes his/her ability to perform the job" (p. 1).

Both parties are claiming ownership over the issue of a teacher's private life and employment status. While exemplar has the longer history of use, nexus, as embodied in the *Morrison* criteria, appears consistently in courts across the nation. The issue will likely be contested into the near future. Because teachers work so closely with the children of the community, they hold a special position of trust and responsibility. That relationship is not given up easily. On the other hand, teachers are not likely to give up the greater latitude of action afforded them with nexus. These opposing views are not easily reconciled. Exemplar without nexus allows the community to be oppressive. Nexus without exemplar subordinates the community to the profession. The courts will likely remain the forum in which each side asserts their position. But are the courts the proper forum for this debate?

Because of the pivotal role educators play in the education of youth and in supporting the moral fabric of the community, this gatekeeper debate must be opened up and expanded. How do the concepts of professionalism, autonomy, accountability, and responsibility factor into the discussion on what standard we use to determine who shall teach our children? Must teachers be mandatory role models in all that they do, even in their private life, or should they be afforded the normal rights of privacy enjoyed by other professionals? The answer is not easy; but nonetheless, the discussion must begin, because who teaches matters. The criteria that we use for placing professionally competent educators in classrooms is important. How we define professional expectations of behavior is crucial to reform.

REFERENCES

Beale, H. K. (1936). *Are American teachers free? An analysis of restraints upon the freedom of teaching in American schools.* New York: Scribner's Sons.

Board of Education of Hopkins County v. Wood, 717 S.W. 2d 837 (1986).

Chicago Board of Education v. Payne, 102 Ill. App. 3d 741 (1981).

DeMitchell, T. A. (1993). *Private Lives: Community Control vs. Professional Autonomy.* 78 Ed. Law Rep. [187] (Jan. 14).

DeMitchell, T. A. and DeMitchell, T. A. (1990). The law in relation to teacher out of school behavior. *Education* 110:381–387.

Elsbree, W. S. 1939. *The American teacher: Evolution of a profession in a democracy.* New York: American Book Company.

Erb v. Iowa State Board of Education of Public Instruction, 216 N.W. 2d 339 (1974).

Fisher v. Snyder, 467 F.2d 375 (8th Cir. 1973).

Green, J. (Ed.) 1986. *What next? More leverage for teachers*. Denver, CO: Education Commission of the States.

Horosko v. School District of Mount Pleasant Township, 6 A.2d 866 (1939).

Jarvella v. Willoughby-Eastlake City School District, 233 N.E. 2d 143 (1967).

Kaestle, C. F. (1983) *Pillars of the republic: Common schools and American society, 1780–1860*. New York: Hill and Wang.

McBroom v. Board of Education, District No. 205, 98 Ill. Dec. 864 (1986).

McElhannon, J. C. (1929). The social failure of the teacher. *The Journal of Educational Sociology*. 2:535–544.

Morrison v. State Board of Education, 82 Cal. Rptr. 175 (1969).

Nolte, M. C. *Establishing a nexus: A school board primer*. 38 Ed. Law Rep. 1.

Perryman v. School Committee of Boston, 458 N.E. 2d 748 (1983).

Scott v. Board of Education of Alton, 156 N.E. 2d 1 (1959).

Tyack, D.B. 1974. *The one-best system: A history of urban education*. Cambridge, MA: Harvard University Press.

Tyack, D. B. and Hansot, E. 1982. *Managers of virtue: Public school leadership in America, 1820–1980*. New York: Basic Books.

Watson v. Board of Education, 99 Cal. Rptr. 468 (1972).

ENDNOTE

1. See Gover v. Stovall, 35 S.W. 2d 24 (1931). Gover, a teacher, was in his school between eight and nine o'clock at night with another man and three young ladies, one of whom was a pupil at the school. They kept the lights off and kept the meeting a secret for several days. Even though there was no immoral act perpetrated or attempted, Gover was dismissed because his conduct invited criticism and produced suspicions of immorality. In Tingley v. Vaughn, (1985), 17 Ill. App. 347, the court wrote: ''If suspicion of vice or immorality be once entertained against a teacher, his influence for good is gone. The parents become distrustful, the pupils contemptuous and school discipline essential to success is at an end'' (p. 351).

CHAPTER 5

Educational Malpractice: Will School Reform Efforts Make It Possible?*

> *Reading is a basic life skill. It is a cornerstone for a child's success in school and, indeed, throughout life.*
>
> —Anderson et al., 1985, p. 1
>
> *The novel — and troublesome — question on this appeal is whether a person who claims to have been inadequately educated, while a student in a public school system, may state a cause of action in tort against the public authorities who operate and administer the system.* We hold that he may not.
>
> —[Peter W. v. San Francisco Unified School District, 60 Cal. App. 3rd 817, 817 (Ct. App. 1976); Emphasis added]

It has been twenty years since the landmark case, *Peter W.* was heard. This case was the first to grapple with the issue of educational malpractice. The court ultimately denied a remedy to the plaintiff, thereby setting a precedent that has been followed in all subsequent educational malpractice cases. However, does the reasoning set forth by the court in *Peter W.* and followed by subsequent courts still apply given recent reform efforts?

Historically, schools have shouldered the responsibility of providing educational opportunities that foster the development of literacy and other necessary skills; however, we know that schools have not always been successful in their mission to educate. According to the results of the National Assessment of Educational Progress, only 39 percent of

*This chapter is authored by Terri A. DeMitchell.

high school seniors are able to read textbooks appropriate to their grade level with understanding (Chall et al., 1990; NAEP, 1989). Furthermore, the statistics regarding the number of adult illiterates in this country are staggering. Estimates range from 27 to 72 million (Chall et al., 1987). While clearly other factors are involved in literacy acquisition, schools certainly must share in the responsibility.

Interestingly, educators have not been held accountable for their role in this serious problem, despite the fact that such unacceptable outcomes are not summarily accepted in other professions. For example, when a physician is sued for negligence, the actions of the physician are scrutinized and the patient is compensated for injuries suffered due to proven professional malpractice. However, if a student receiving a public education is not adequately educated, the injured student will not be compensated.

The reasons for this refusal center around both legal issues and public policy issues. Legal issues include difficulty in establishing the elements of a tort, such as determining that a duty is owed by an educator to a student, recognizing a standard of care in education, and proving that a breach of the standard of care caused an injury to the student. Policy issues include a policy of noninterference by the courts in educational matters and the belief that allowing such suits to be brought will open the floodgates of litigation, resulting in a burden to our school systems.

As the educational community struggles with reform efforts to increase its professional stature, the discussion of educational malpractice becomes imperative. Our reform efforts are seeking to define norms for professional practice. The closer these efforts come to a reality, the greater the likelihood these standards of educational practice will be used to judge the competence of the educator. Professional practice and its twin, malpractice, may be at the end of the reform equation. Cooper (1988) succinctly states the issue when she writes: "Malpractice implies the presence of a standard of practice against which to measure professional judgments. We will know that teaching is a profession when a malpractice suit becomes plausible" (p. 52). Therefore, it is time to revisit educational malpractice in light of recent reform efforts.

PROFESSIONAL MALPRACTICE

Professionals who allegedly have engaged in professional misconduct or who allegedly lack appropriate skills may be sued for malpractice. Malpractice is often distinguished from other wrongs committed by professionals, in that it deals with the quality of the services rendered (Mallen, 1979). Generally, malpractice actions are brought under tort law.

A tort is a civil wrong other than a breach of contract. Under tort law, an individual who has suffered because of the improper conduct of another may sue that person for money damages. The purpose of tort law is to balance a plaintiff's claim to protection from damages against a defendant's freedom of action. Often, the potential social consequences of a particular judicial determination will be examined when deciding a case. Thus, in tort litigation, even if it is appropriate to provide a remedy to a specific plaintiff, it is possible that the plaintiff will be denied a remedy if it is determined that there may be negative social consequences associated with such a decision (Prosser & Keeton, 1984). These social consequences are sometimes referred to as public policy concerns. As will be discussed, public policy concerns play a significant role in malpractice litigation.

Tort actions for malpractice are brought under the theory of negligence if the acts of the professional that allegedly inflicted harm were not intended to cause harm. Since most harmful acts by professionals are unintentional, the most common theory for malpractice asserted against a professional is negligence. To successfully bring an action under the theory of negligence, the following elements must be present and proven by the plaintiff:

(1) A legal duty to conform to a certain standard of conduct
(2) A failure to conform to the standard required
(3) A causal connection between the conduct and the resulting injury
(4) Actual loss or damage resulting from the breach of duty (Prosser & Keeton, 1984)

To more clearly understand the reasons for the differing results reached by the courts with respect to professional malpractice cases involving negligence, examples of judicial determinations for both physicians and educators will be reviewed, highlighting the legal and policy issues involved.

LEGAL ISSUES

Duty

The first element required in any negligence case is the existence of a duty owed by the defendant to the complaining party. Whether a defendant owes a duty to a plaintiff is a question of whether or not the defendant is under a legal obligation to act or not to act for the benefit of the plaintiff. The courts readily recognize such a duty between a physician and patient for policy reasons. It is easy to understand why. Patients often stake their lives on the belief that they will receive competent care when they seek medical assistance. This duty applies to all aspects of the relationship from diagnosis to treatment.

A duty of care will arise between a physician and a patient if there is a contract for professional services. Therefore, if a physician and a patient agree that in exchange for a fee, the physician will treat the patient, an express contract will be created. In most instances, however, a physician and patient do not enter into such negotiations. Instead, a patient simply enters the physician's office and receives treatment. Under these circumstances, the courts recognize that an implied contract is created if a physician treats a patient with the expectation of compensation. This is true regardless of who pays for the treatment (Prosser & Keeton, 1984).

Statutes may also create a duty. Some states have required that hospitals with emergency facilities render emergency care (Cal. Health & Safety Code Section 1317). Even without express statutes, some courts have found that licensing statutes and health regulations require that emergency care facilities treat emergency patients, thus creating a duty [*Guerrero v. Cooper Queen Hospital* (1975)].

Furthermore, physicians can be held liable under the theory of vicarious liability for the negligent acts of their employees if the acts occurred within the scope of employment (Prosser & Keeton, 1984). Therefore, if a nurse negligently injures a patient while giving the patient an injection, the physician can be held liable. It is obvious from this that the courts readily find a duty of care has arisen when the case involves professionals such as physicians.

In the landmark case *Peter W. v. San Francisco Unified School District* (1976), the issue of educational malpractice was first adjudicated. This case set the stage for all subsequent educational malpractice actions by clearly denying recovery. In this case, a high school graduate brought suit against the San Francisco Unified School District, the superintendent, and governing board to recover for alleged negligence in instruction and intentional misrepresentation of the student's progress. The plaintiff claimed that these actions resulted in depriving him of basic academic skills. The court found that the San Francisco Unified School District did not owe Peter W. a duty of due care. In other words, the court found that the teachers and the administrators had no duty to educate Peter W. The reasons given by the court included a concern that finding a cause of action would expose districts to tort claims in countless numbers, which would burden the school systems; a belief that no standard of care exists because there is no recognized methodology in education; and the difficulty in determining why a student has failed to acquire basic academic skills. Thus the court determined that, since it would be difficult to establish the elements of a legal cause of action in tort, such as breach of duty, causation, and damages, and because of the policy concern of overburdening school districts, no duty of due care be found.

A subsequent case, *Donohue v. Copiague Union Free School District* (1979), also found that a duty of care was not owed to a high school graduate who alleged that he was not adequately educated. In this case, the court concluded that, for policy reasons, a duty was not owed. The court determined that it should not interfere with the control and management of schools since statutory law gave control to local school boards. Thus, the courts believe that educators should not be held accountable for the services they render, for both legal and policy reasons.

Breach of Duty of Due Care

Mere dissatisfaction with the services rendered, however, is not enough for a successful claim against a professional, even if a duty is established. There must be a breach of the duty of care, which involves the establishment of the degree of care owed, and proof that the defendant did not meet the requisite standard.

The degree of care owed by the professional must be established at trial. Generally, proof of the requisite standard of care is determined by the testimony of expert witnesses knowledgeable about established and acceptable standards and, in the case of a physician, knowledgeable about the medical condition in question [*Swanson v. Chatterton* (1968)]. This is true unless the requisite level of care is apparent to a lay juror. However, as will be shown, the standard of care for physicians is defined very generally since the courts recognize that medicine is not a precise science. Therefore, critically analyzing the facts of each situation becomes the focal point in litigation.

For physicians, the standard of care that is owed to a patient can be established by state statute by professional standards. Whether a violation of a standard conclusively establishes a breach of the standard of care is open to debate. In determining whether a physician has breached the requisite standard of care, several factors are examined. These factors include the state of professional knowledge at the time of the act or omission by the physician and established modes of practice. The professional knowledge requirement recognizes that medical service is a progressive science, and therefore, treatment rendered must be evaluated in light of the knowledge at the time in question. In addition, physicians are not held liable for mistakes in judgment where the proper action is open to debate [*Creasey v. Hogan* (1981); *Becker v. Hidalgo* (1976)].

Conversely, no standard of care has been found in education. In *Peter W.* (1976), the court stated that classroom methodology affords no acceptable standard of care. To support its findings, the court pointed to conflicting theories regarding how and what to teach students, but did not cite references for its conclusions.

In *Hoffman v. Board of Education of the City of New York* (1979), a case involving a special education student, similar concerns were expressed regarding the lack of a standard of care. In this case, the court voiced concern that, whenever a student failed to progress, it could be argued that he or she would have progressed if another form of instruction or assessment had been used.

Contrary conclusions have been reached, however. In *Donohue* (1979), even though the court found that no duty of care exists, the court declared that it did not think that the creation of a standard of care, with which an educator's performance could be measured, would present an insurmountable obstacle. In addition, a dissenting opinion in *Hunter v. Board of Education of Montgomery County* (1982), though not a binding opinion, concluded that, since educators receive special training and are state certified, they possess special skills and knowledge and should use customary care. Therefore, due to conflicting viewpoints, it is possible that a court could find that a standard of care exists in education.

Causation

However, proof that a duty of care exists, coupled with a showing that the defendant breached that duty, does not necessarily mean that a plaintiff will recover. The plaintiff must prove that he or she was injured and that the injury sustained was actually and proximately caused by the defendant's negligence.

A physician cannot be held liable, even if negligent, if the negligent actions did not, in fact, cause the injury that the plaintiff claims to have suffered. For example, a physician who negligently prescribed a decongestant for a patient with heart disease could not be held liable for the patient's subsequent heart attack without proof that the medication contributed to the patient's death [*Fall v. White* (1983)]. Furthermore, the defendant's negligence must be the proximate cause of the plaintiff's injuries. In other words, the injury must be a foreseeable result of the physician's action or inaction.

Establishing causation has also been a major stumbling block in education cases. In *Peter W.* (1976), the court stated that the achievement or failure of a student in literacy development is influenced by numerous factors beyond the education received, thus making causation difficult to establish. These factors include physical, neurological, emotional, cultural, and environmental factors. The *Donohue* (1979) court supplemented this list with the following factors: student attitude, motivation, temperament, past experiences, and home environment; however, the court in *Donohue* (1979) acknowledged that while proving causation might be difficult, even impossible in some instances, it assumes too much to conclude that causation could never be established. In addition, a dissenting opinion in *Hoffman* (1979) concluded that the failure by school officials to follow a recommendation for reevaluation of the plaintiff, which resulted in his misplacement into a CRMD class, was readily identifiable as the proximate cause of the plaintiff's injury.

Again, the courts do not rule out the possibility of establishing causation in educational malpractice cases.

Injury

Even if all of the elements of negligence are established at trial, this will not ensure that the defendant will be compensated. The plaintiff must have actually suffered an injury because of the negligent act. Therefore, even a physician who commits a negligent act will not be held liable if the patient is not injured. For example, the courts have refused to award damages to women who seek abortions that are unsuccessful, resulting in the birth of a healthy child. The courts are unwilling to regard the birth of a healthy infant as an injury [*Nanke v. Napier* (1984)]. However, a court will provide a remedy to an injured patient if it is shown that the physician acted in a negligent manner.

With respect to educators, the courts have been divided about whether or not injury can be established in education cases. The court in *Peter W.* (1976) contended that there was no certainty that the plaintiff suffered any injury within the legal definition of negligence despite negligent acts by the defendants; and in *Hunter* (1979), the court reiterated the concern that there is an inherent uncertainty in determining damages. However, the court in *Hunter* (1974) opined that, if a tort of educational malpractice was recognized, money damages would be a poor remedy, thus suggesting that a limitation of damages would be appropriate. Once again, the dissent in *Hunter* (1979) points out the feasibility of an action in educational malpractice by stating that there can be no question that a negligent educator may damage a child. Therefore, the courts have not precluded the possibility of establishing injury in educational malpractice cases.

Defenses

If the plaintiff has contributed to his or her injuries or has assumed some sort of risk, damages will not be awarded or will be reduced. The courts have held that the creation of a physician-patient relationship requires that the duty established be reciprocal. Thus, the patient is required to use the care a person would ordinarily use in similar circumstances, and if he or she does not, then the patient cannot hold the physician liable for harm. Specifically, a patient is required to provide adequate information to the physician, follow the instructions given by the physician, and submit to the treatment the physician orders. If failure to do so enhances the injury, the patient will not be able to recover damages for his or her contribution to the injury. For example, in an action against a physician for the improper diagnosis of appendicitis, the court held the plaintiff contributorily negligent for failing to disclose pertinent information to the physician and for failing to seek further medical attention when her condition worsened [*Carreker v. Harper* (1990)].

Since educational malpractice is not recognized as a cause of action, the issue of defenses has not been addressed in the case law. However, discussion of factors regarding causation, such as motivation and home life discussed previously, could be raised as defenses since these are external factors beyond the control of the educator. The classic defense of contributory negligence on the part of the plaintiff would probably be available in an educational malpractice suit. This defense could be raised when the student failed to follow the instructions of the teacher, such as not turning in assignments or turning in partially completed assignments, or when a student failed to pay attention in class. Therefore, a student would arguably be required to take reasonable responsibility for his or her own learning.

POLICY ISSUES

In addition to the legal issues, policy issues also play a critical role in the decision to not recognize educational malpractice as a cause of action. As stated previously, policy issues can completely close off a legal analysis such as when policy considerations preclude the recognition of a duty. Currently, public policy dictates that medical malpractice be recognized as a cause of action but that educational malpractice not be recognized. However, policy is ever changing, and therefore, a look at public policy as it relates to education is essential.

For years, school districts were immune from tort liability, regardless of the circumstances surrounding the claim against the district. This was based on a common law principle that the government could not be sued without its consent. The policy reasons that were given for protecting school districts were: 1) school districts have only the powers granted by the legislature, and if the legislature did not give the school districts the power to be sued, they could not be sued; 2) since the public would receive no benefit from allowing successful suits, payment of damages from school district funds would be an illegal expenditure of public funds; 3) allowing suits would open the floodgates and place a financial burden on school districts; 4) the concept of respondeat superior, which allows an employer to be sued for the actions of his or her employees, does not apply to school districts; and 5) immunity cannot be abolished by the judiciary, but only by the legislature (Alexander & Alexander, 1984).

However, a change in attitude regarding the appropriateness of governmental immunity with regard to school districts resulted in change in both policy and law. In *Molitor v. Kaneland Community Unit District No. 302* (1959), the court found that a school district could be held liable in a tort action. In this case, a student was injured in a school bus accident. In overturning existing policy that granted immunity, the court stated that it was almost incredible that the concept of governmental immunity could exempt governmental entities from liability for their tortious acts that resulted in a burden to an individual.

Today, school districts are held liable for many of their negligent actions. Generally, such actions are associated with physical injuries suffered by students. In these instances, the courts have little trouble with the issue of negligence. For example, liability was found when a second-grade teacher placed an uncovered lit candle on her desk, which set fire to a costume a student was wearing for a school play [*Smith v. Archbishop of St. Louis* (1982)]. In another case, school personnel were found liable for negligent supervision when two high school boys were slap-boxing in an unsupervised area. One boy died when he fell backwards and hit his head [*Daily v. Los Angeles Unified School District* (1970)].

While liability can be found in instances of negligence that involve physical harm, thus far, there have been no successful cases brought on behalf of a student for educational malpractice under a theory of negligence. The public policy reasons surrounding this decision are not unlike those asserted to support governmental immunity; however, as shown, public policy can change.

One of the reasons cited by the courts for not recognizing a duty of care is the history of noninterference by the courts in educational matters. In *Hoffman* (1979) the court stated that it should not substitute its judgment or the judgment of a jury for the professional judgment of educators, except in instances of gross violations of public policy. The courts in *Donohue* (1979) and *Hunter* (1982) added that the participation in school matters would interfere with the authority vested in school officials to oversee the schools.

The other policy reason for refusing to recognize a cause of action for educational malpractice is a concern that the floodgates of litigation would be opened if such a cause of action were possible, resulting in a burden to school systems. In *Peter W.* (1976), the court expressed great concern regarding the ramifications of recognizing a duty of due care in education. The court pointed out that schools have already aroused controversy and dissatisfaction due to a perceived failure to achieve educational expectations; therefore, recognizing a cause of action for educational malpractice would burden the schools financially due to the large numbers of disgruntled students and parents that would attempt to sue. The court in *Hunter* (1982) also pointed out that such a cause of action would place an extreme burden on public school resources.

SCHOOL REFORM AND EDUCATIONAL MALPRACTICE

As discussed, a duty of care owed by educators to students has not been found for both policy reasons and legal reasons. These reasons are often intertwined with concerns regarding one aspect governing decisions regarding another. However, we also know that the courts have suggested that a cause of action for malpractice is not out of the realm of possibility. For this reason, it is important to look at the effect school reform efforts might have on current policy and law.

The two policy considerations that have surfaced most often can be addressed. The concern that the judiciary does not become involved in school matters is arguably not true. The courts have been involved with cases that fall short of gross violations of public policy such as overturning board policies regarding a student's hair [*Arnold v. Carpenter* (1972)] and instructional decisions such as determining the appropriateness of teaching a foreign language [*Meyer v. Nebraska* (1923)].

With respect to the concern that school districts will be financially burdened, the damages can easily be limited to compensatory damages such as providing additional schooling for the plaintiff. In fact, such damages would be more appropriate given that the judiciary would strive to make the plaintiff whole. However, if money damages were allowed, they too could be limited.

The remaining issues have been significant stumbling blocks in efforts to have a cause of action for educational malpractice recognized. However, these issues have been and will continue to be addressed by school reform efforts. The remaining concerns include determining that a standard of care exists in education and establishing causation between negligent actions by an educator and injury to a student. Clearly, the first wave of reform created a number of mandates that revised certification and training for teachers. It also established assessment standards and graduation requirements. While these mandates have not actually created a statutory duty to educate with due care, they certainly suggest that there is a certain level of competence that can be identifed for both teachers and students. This would appear to be strengthened by a review of state laws that mandate that teachers, as a condition of retaining their teaching certificates, participate in an established number of hours of professional activities. As districts more closely evaluate teachers and students, causal connections between student performance and teacher competence may become easier to link.

In addition, as the second wave of reform promotes greater professional control of education, issues such as establishing a standard of care may also be resolved. As the profession dictates more policy and procedures, a standard of care may be established by the profession, whether it intends to establish such a standard or not. Thus, school reform may provide the missing link that will enable a cause of action for educational malpractice to be recognized.

REFERENCES

Alexander, K. and Alexander, M. D. (1984). *The law of schools, students, and teachers in a nutshell.* St. Paul: West Publishing Company.

Anderson, R. C., Hiebert, E. H., Scott, J. A., and Wilkinson, I. A. G. (1985). *Becoming a nation of readers: The report of the Commission on Reading.* Washington, D.C.: National Institute of Education.

Arnold v. Carpenter, 459 F.2d 939 (7th Cir., 1972).

Becker v. Hidalgo, 89 N.M. 627, 556 P.2d 35 (1976).

Carreker v. Harper, 196 Ga. App. 658, 396 S.E.2d 587 (1990).

Chall, J., Heron, E. and Hilferty, A. (1987). Adult literacy: New and enduring problems. *Phi Delta Kappan* 69:190–196.

Chall, J. S., Jacobs, V. A., and Baldwin, L. E. (1990). *The reading crisis: Why poor children fall behind.* Cambridge: Harvard University Press and National Assessment of Educational Progress.

Cooper, M. (1988) Whose culture is it anyway? In A. Lieberman (Ed.), *Building a professional culture in schools.* New York: Teachers College Press.

Creasey v. Hogan, 292 Or. 154, 637 P.2d 114 (1981).

Daily v. Los Angeles Unified School District, 87 Cal. Rptr. 376 (1970).

Donohue v. Copiague Union Free School District, 391 N.E.2d 1352 (N.Y., 1979).

Fall v. White, 449 N.E.2d 635 (Ind. App., 1983).

Guerrero v. Cooper Queen Hospital, 112 Ariz. 104, 537 P.2d 1329 (1975).

Hoffman v. Board of Education of the City of New York, 400 N.E.2d 317 (N.Y., 1979).

Hunter v. Board of Education of Montgomery County, 439 A.2d 582 (Md., 1982).

Mallen, *Recognizing and Defending Legal Malpractice,* 30 S.C. L. REV. 203 (1979).

Meyer v. Nebraska, 262 U.S. 390, 43 S.Ct. 625 (1923).

Molitor v. Kaneland Community Unit District No. 302, 18 Ill.2d 11, 163 N.E.2d 89 (1959).

Nanke v. Napier, 346 N.W.2d 520 (Iowa, 1984).

National Assessment of Educational Progress, (1989). Princeton, NJ: Educational Testing Service.

Prosser, W. L. and Keeton, W. P. (1984). *Prosser and Keeton on torts* (5th edition). St. Paul, Minn: West Publishing Co.

Smith v. Archbishop of St. Louis, 632 S.W.2d 516 (Mo., 1982).

Swanson v. Chatterton, 281 Minn. 129, 160 N.W.2d 662 (1968).

PART THREE

CLASSROOM OR WORKPLACE: WHOSE PLACE IS IT?

CHAPTER 6

From Sunnyvale to Flatbush: The Conflict between School Reform and Teachers' Job Protections

> *Nobility is defined by the demands it makes upon us — by obligations, not by rights.*
>
> —Jose Ortega y Gasset

The most recent American school reform movement is now more than fifteen years old, and it is has introduced a bewildering array of educational innovations. Site-based management, charter schools, teacher performance standards, pupil accountability schemes, school choice, merit-based pay plans, and total quality management are just a few of the reforms that have been introduced into American schools since 1980. Two commentators have estimated that more than 700 individual reform initiatives have been implemented (Timar & Kirp, 1988). One reform bill alone, the Massachusetts Education Reform Act of 1993, included more than fifty separate school reform provisions.

Unfortunately, in spite of all the law-making, public education has changed very little. As William Clune (1993) has written, "The United States produces the largest quantity of educational policy in the world, and the least effective" (p. 125). Even teachers' union leaders, who would seem to have an interest in putting the best face on the state of public education, are deeply pessimistic about the state of American schools. "Our public schools are in deep trouble," AFT president Albert Shanker wrote in 1992, "but that's hardly news" (p. 3).

Although there are many reasons for this state of affairs, one partial

77

explanation has largely been overlooked. Few have noticed that while state legislators have been busily passing reform initiatives to improve schools, they failed to examine the strong job protection laws that have been passed in most states for the benefit of teachers and administrators. Taken together, these job protection laws have woven a thick safety net against discipline or dismissal, a net so strong that even educators who commit serious acts of misconduct are often able to maintain contact with school children.

This development can be described in many ways, but the scope of the problem is well illustrated by a California court case, decided in 1980, when the school reform movement was in first bloom. The decision chronicles the efforts of Sunnyvale Elementary School District to fire a teacher after he was convicted of falsely reporting that a bomb had been planted in the school where he worked as a teacher of retarded children.

According to the court decision, the teacher telephoned the bomb threat during a teachers' strike, in the belief that a visual count of evacuating students would challenge the school district's report of student attendance levels. The teacher was arrested after school employees identified his voice in a tape recording of the threat. He later pled no contest to a charge of falsely reporting that a bomb or explosive device had been planted, and he served seven days in jail.

In the wake of these events, the Sunnyvale school district tried to discharge the teacher for unprofessional and immoral conduct. In accordance with California law, three individuals were impaneled as a Commission of Professional Competence. The panel decided that the conduct did not justify dismissal, and the school district appealed. A California trial court not only upheld the Commission's decision, it also awarded the teacher $7,000 in attorney's fees.

Sunnyvale school district then appealed this decision to the California Court of Appeals, where it argued that the act of falsely reporting an explosive device in a school was so shocking and outrageous that the teacher was unfit to teach as a matter of law. Here, the school district found a somewhat sympathetic tribunal. Indeed, the court began its analysis by endorsing an arbitration decision's censor of such conduct:

> We view the phoning in of bomb threats as one of the lowest forms of human activity, roughly equivalent to arson and rape. They are similar because in all three situations, an individual is willing to jeopardize the interests of others — perhaps even the lives of others — for his own imme-

diate gratification. (*Board of Education of Sunnyvale Elementary School District v. Commission on Professional Competence*, 1980, p. 593, citing *Eastern Associated Coal Co.*, 1976).

Nevertheless, the California appellate court reluctantly concluded that the teacher should be retained in the classroom. Under California law, the court observed, courts are required to uphold lower courts' findings of fact if they are supported by substantial evidence. Since there was substantial evidence that the teacher retained effective classroom control, had the support of faculty and students, and continued to be an effective teacher, the administrative decision was affirmed. In addition, the court required the school district to pay the teacher's attorney fees.

The *Sunnyvale* case is remarkable for two reasons. First, it demonstrates our society's high tolerance for people who behave inappropriately with school children. It seems unlikely that a member of any other profession—law, medicine, accounting, or nursing—could telephone a bomb threat to his workplace and keep his job.

Second, *Sunnyvale* illustrates the legal hurdles a school district must surmount to remove a teacher for misconduct, even in cases that a layperson would interpret as straightforward and clear-cut. In spite of the fact that a teacher had been convicted of a very serious criminal offense involving the workplace, the school district was forced to pursue dismissal before three separate tribunals. In the end, all three tribunals held for the school teacher, and the school district was required to pay the teacher's legal fees, in addition to its own.

Of course, the Sunnyvale case is unusual, but it is not unique. In 1994, *The New York Times* reported that a New York City school teacher arrested for selling cocaine in 1989 still had his job four years later (Dillon, 1994). The teacher, who had been assigned to a school in the Flatbush section of Brooklyn, pled guilty to felony drug charges in June 1990 and was sentenced to serve two to six years in prison.

According to *The New York Times,* the teacher continued to draw his salary while he was incarcerated. School district dismissal proceedings did not begin until 1991. Eight hearing sessions stretched over a period of ten months. Not until May 1992, three years after his arrest, was he formally discharged.

Even then, the New York City schools were not free of this individual. The teacher appealed his dismissal to the New York Commissioner of Education, who reduced the penalty to two years' suspension without pay. After the suspension period ended in May 1994, the teacher demanded his job back, claiming he had been rehabilitated.

SHORTCOMINGS

Although Sunnyvale and Flatbush are extreme cases, they illustrate three serious problems with the way American school districts deal with teachers who are accused of misconduct. First, in some jurisdictions, school boards have been relieved of the ultimate responsibility for disciplining incompetent and misbehaving teachers. In these states, school boards' dismissal decisions can be countermanded by arbitrators or administrative officers who are often more sympathetic than school boards to misbehaving teachers. Second, teacher disciplinary proceedings have become inordinately complex, time-consuming, and expensive. Often, teacher dismissal proceedings take place in an Alice-in-Wonderland atmosphere where lawyers and advocates argue endlessly about legal technicalities that have little to do with the welfare of children. Third, complex discipline procedures discourage school decision makers from discharging incompetent or immoral teachers.

Taken together, these shortcomings are a hindrance to school reform. No matter how wise and creative our school reform initiatives may be, they must be implemented by educators in the field, and if those educators are indifferent, incompetent, or even immoral, it is very difficult to remove them.

School boards are losing their authority to discharge unsatisfactory teachers.

First, school boards are losing their authority to remove unsatisfactory teachers. Although boards may make the initial decision to remove a teacher, in many states, that decision can be reversed by an independent tribunal, usually a statutory administrative body or an arbitrator.

In California, for example, when a school board terminates a tenured teacher, a commission on professional competence is impaneled to decide if the dismissal is justified. Each commission is made up of three members. One member is chosen by the school board; the teacher chooses one; and one member is assigned by a state agency (Calif. Educ.

Code § 44944). In several jurisdictions, a school district's dismissal charges are heard by a single arbitrator — generally an attorney — with the teacher having some role in determining which arbitrator will be selected.

Often, these reviewing bodies are more sympathetic than school boards to teachers accused of wrongdoing. Since the arbitrator must be acceptable to both the school district and the teacher, a teacher is much more likely to get friendly treatment in arbitration than he or she would have gotten in a hearing before the school committee. As two commentators noted, "The arbitrator's acceptability . . . is largely a function of his awards, which must neither wholly please nor wholly displease a party" (Finch & Nagel, 1984, p. 1651).

Moreover, many of the arbitrators who review school discipline decisions are labor lawyers with little experience in an educational environment. Often, they analyze school disciplinary proceedings the same way they would analyze a labor dispute between blue-collar workers and factory owners. They frequently do not understand the educational implications of their decisions, nor are they sensitive to the need for collegiality and professionalism in the workplace.

A couple of court cases illustrate the way school boards and reviewing tribunals can disagree about what constitutes just cause for dismissal. In a California case, a school board attempted to fire a teacher after discovering that she had worked at two other schools for more than a year while taking sick leave from the district. The teacher argued that she had relied on the advice of a union representative and a union lawyer that what she was doing was not illegal. A commission of professional competence, impaneled to hear the charges, unanimously agreed that the teacher had acted honestly and should be reinstated.

A California court, however, took a commonsense approach to the case and reversed the commission. Obviously, the court reasoned, the teacher could not have had a sincere belief that she was unable to work since she did, in fact, work at two teaching jobs during the time she was on sick leave (*Bassett Unified School District v. Commission on Professional Competence*, 1988, p. 870). The court set aside the commission's finding that the teacher had acted honestly and approved the school board's dismissal decision.

Similarly, in a Pennsylvania case, an appellate court reversed an arbitrator who ruled that a school district could not dismiss two teachers who had taken sick leave to go on a ski trip. According to the court decision, the teachers had asked for personal leave for the days in question, but the superintendent had denied their request. They went on the ski trip anyway, requested sick leave, and backed up their request with a letter from a psychologist stating that both teachers were suffering from stress. An arbitrator ruled that the sick leave requests were justified, and a trial court reluctantly affirmed the arbitrator's decision.

A Pennsylvania appellate court, like the California appellate court, agreed with the school board's assessment of the teachers' conduct. Misrepresentations about unexcused absences are a proper subject of immorality charges, the court ruled. Based on the record, the teachers' conduct provided just cause for dismissal. Accordingly, the court reversed the arbitrator and reinstated the school district's dismissal actions (*Riverview School District v. Riverview Education Association,* 1994).

Of course, arbitrators and administrative review panels do not always countermand school board dismissal proceedings; in many instances, they are affirmed. And these reviewing bodies often serve a useful purpose by providing an objective and detached perspective in cases where school boards fire teachers arbitrarily, without sufficient evidence, or based on political motivations.

Nevertheless, it is quite significant that legislatures around the country have taken the ultimate power to discipline or dismiss teachers away from school boards and given it to administrative officers or arbitrators. Often, these reviewers have a vested interest in pleasing teachers' groups, or they fail to appreciate the educational implications of school board's personnel decisions.

Teacher dismissal proceedings are unduly complex, time-consuming, and expensive.

Second, teacher dismissal proceedings are often unduly time-consuming, complex, and expensive. Indeed, although the public often criticizes the criminal courts for unnecessary delays in administering justice, many people would be surprised to learn that the criminal justice system often acts more swiftly than teacher dismissal proceedings. For example, the Flatbush teacher who was charged with selling cocaine in May 1989 was imprisoned in July 1990, fourteen months later. A hearing panel, however, did not get around to firing him for the offense until May 1992, three years after his arrest (Dillon, 1994). In the Sunnyvale case, a California appellate court issued its ruling in February 1980, about forty months after the conduct that led to the teacher's discharge. And in a recent Louisiana case, an appellate court did not rule on a school board's dismissal of a bus driver until almost nine years after the board's original decision (*Bernard v. Avoyelles Parish School Board,* 1994).

Not only do teacher discipline cases take a long time to resolve, they are often quite expensive. The New York City School District spent $185,000 in dismissal hearings to remove the Flatbush teacher. Though one might think that his criminal conviction for selling drugs would make the case a simple one, the administrative hearings took 800 pages to transcribe. In a recent Connecticut case, a school district spent nearly a quarter of a million dollars trying to discharge a tenured teacher without bringing the matter to resolution. The administrative hearing in that case lasted twenty-nine days and produced a 5,000-page transcript and 400 exhibits (Frahm, 1994). According to a study by the state's school boards association, the average cost of a New York teacher dismissal proceeding, including the cost of a suspended teacher's salary, is almost $200,000 and takes more than a year to conclude (Goldberg, 1994).

One reason that teacher dismissal proceedings are so expensive is that school districts usually continue to pay an accused teacher, pending the outcome of administrative hearings. This process may consume several months or even years. Recently, a Washington school teacher accused of immorality remained on paid leave for two years while the school district pursued dismissal through an administrative process and the courts (Erwin, 1994).

Because they continue to get paid until the administrative hearings are concluded, accused teachers have little incentive to speed up the disciplinary process. On the contrary, they may even deliberately delay the process for this reason (Cortines & Stancik, 1994).

Moreover, protracted litigation over teacher dismissals frequently involves legal technicalities that have little to do with the core issue — a teacher's competence or moral standards. In an Alaska case, for example, a school board dismissed a teacher based on evidence that he physically and verbally abused another teacher in front of school-children. After a jury trial, an Alaskan court upheld the dismissal. The teacher appealed to the state supreme court, where he argued that jury instructions were defective and that the jury had improperly been shown a certain exhibit. Ultimately, the teacher lost his appeal, but the supreme court's decision wasn't rendered until more than five years after the events that triggered his dismissal (*Renfroe v. Green,* 1980).

More recently, a Washington court reversed a school board's decision to demote a principal who allegedly failed to report a case of suspected child abuse against a sixth-grade girl by a school employee. Although the principal received a due-process hearing after his demotion, the court ruled that the district had failed to provide due process *before* the demotion, as required by state law. Consequently, the demotion was ineffective (*J. N. v. Bellingham School District No. 501,* 1994). (However, the court ruled that the dispute was moot, since the school district had validly notified the principal that his contract as principal would not be renewed.)

Of course, teachers deserve the right to put forth all valid defenses to a dismissal charge and to avail themselves of reasonable procedural rights. Nevertheless, once a fair tribunal has determined that a teacher has physically abused another teacher, failed to report suspected child abuse by a school employee, or been convicted of a serious criminal offense, the final outcome in a dismissal proceeding should be swift and sure. No one's legitimate interest is served by dragging on these proceedings for months and years.

Complex discipline procedures discourage school decision makers from discharging incompetent staff members.

Not surprisingly, the almost impenetrable briar patch of teachers' job protection rights and the prospect of protracted litigation often discourages schools from removing immoral, incompetent, and uninspired teachers from the classroom. Unless they engage in very serious criminal misbehavior, tenured school teachers are virtually assured of a lifetime job.

For example, in Connecticut, a state with more than 30,000 certificated teachers, administrators, and social workers, only thirty-seven people had their certificates revoked in a ten-year period (Condon, 1993). In Louisiana, where 44 percent of the state's students do not graduate on time (Annie E. Casey Foundation, 1994), only eighty-eight of 30,000 teachers were rated unsatisfactory in 1993–1994 (Myers,

1994). In the Philadelphia school district, where 25 percent of the first graders are retained in grade, just ten of the district's 10,000 teachers were rated unsatisfactory in 1992–1993 (Schmidt, 1994). And in Boston, a school district with more than 4,000 teachers, virtually no one was dismissed for performance reasons during a ten-year period. A former personnel director of the Boston system admitted, ''We may have gone ten years where the only permanent teachers dismissed were those who were child molesters'' (Wilson, 1992, p. 295).

Rather than initiate the complex and expensive legal processes that accompany discipline and discharge, school administrators often prefer to simply transfer a nonperforming teacher to another site or accept a resignation. Susan Moore Johnson's classic Harvard teaching case, ''The Case of Edna Wiley'' (1978), chronicles the way a school district transferred a seriously deficient teacher from one school to another for many years, rather than confront behavior that was detrimental to children. Another Harvard teaching case describes the way an Alaska school district permitted a teacher accused of sexual misconduct to retire quietly, rather than face dismissal (Fossey & Merseth, 1991).

IS THE PRESENT MEANS OF DISCHARGING TEACHERS SUCH A BAD THING?

Apologists for the present system for disciplining teachers might argue that the current state of affairs is quite satisfactory. First, they may say, some fair and orderly procedure for determining whether a teacher is unfit for the classroom is required by constitutional due process. Thus, we should not complain if due process involves a certain amount of time and expense.

But defenders of the status quo would be wrong if they believe that our cumbersome teacher dismissal procedures are required by the Constitution. Our Constitution guarantees fair procedures for a teacher charged with misconduct: notice of charges, a right to present a defense, and a fair decision maker; however, the Constitution does not require that accused teachers be able to participate in the selection of their tribunals.

More to the point, the Constitution does not require teacher dismissal proceedings to be so time-consuming, expensive, and risk-fraught that school decision makers are reluctant to take action against grossly incompetent or immoral educators. That is a situation that was created by legislatures, administrative agencies, and the educational community; and it is a situation that can well be remedied if the educational community chooses to do so.

Status quo defenders might also argue that the present system places an appropriate value on a teacher's career. There should be a quality of mercy in teacher dismissal proceedings, they might say, a quality that weighs extenuating circumstances and examines single lapses of conduct in the light of entire professional careers. The Sunnyvale teacher, for example, apparently committed one act of poor judgment that blemished an otherwise satisfactory employment record, and the Flatbush teacher, although imprisoned for selling drugs, may well have been rehabilitated.

Nevertheless, by allowing such teachers back in the classroom, society may be paying a high price. As Emile Durkheim observed, the purpose of punishment is not to exact a quid pro quo on a wrongdoer, but for society to exhibit a "passionate reaction" to a violation of community values and customs. In other words, punishment serves to reaffirm the community's central moral beliefs. To permit deviate behavior to go unpunished, Durkheim believed, creates a social "illness" (Nisbet, 1974, pp. 222–224).

Perhaps, if Durkheim is right, our present cumbersome and ineffective system for disciplining wayward teachers plays some part in the failure of school reform to revitalize our schools. A society that fails to remove convicted drug dealers and reporters of false bomb threats has lost its power of "passionate reaction" with regard to its children's environment. If we will tolerate the Sunnyvale teacher and the Flatbush teacher in our schools, we will tolerate a very wide range of misbehavior.

Moreover, if even a small fraction of the nation's teachers are unsatisfactory or immoral, their presence in the classroom can have enormously bad consequences. As Edwin Bridges has pointed out, if only 4 percent of the nation's teachers are incompetent, their numbers would represent the entire teaching force in our twelve smallest states (Bridges, 1988).

WHAT SHOULD BE DONE?

Although the education community has not come to grips with this issue, the public has a clear sense that a high tolerance for incompetent and deviate teachers contributes to a decline in the quality of our schools.

It is not surprising, then, that a recurring theme of school reform is the need to develop better mechanisms for removing poor teachers from the classroom. Teacher competency examinations, rigorous evaluation standards, and tenure revision ideas are just some of the proposals that have been tried to improve the quality of the teaching force.

Unfortunately, few of these ideas have met with much success. In Louisiana, the state legislature passed the Children First Act in 1988, which required all Louisiana teachers to submit to uniform state-sponsored evaluations. Teachers' interest groups rallied and basically dismantled the law (Maxcy & Maxcy, 1993). The local evaluations that have been done since then determined that less than one-tenth of 1 percent of Louisiana teachers were unsatisfactory. In Massachusetts, Governor William Weld declared that a central goal of the Massachusetts Education Reform Act would be to remove unreasonable restrictions on removing bad tenured teachers. But after the MERA was passed, the governor acknowledged that the new law had probably made it harder, not easier, to remove unsatisfactory tenured teachers (Howe, 1993).

Edwin Bridges (1988) has urged school districts to pay more attention to the tenure process, thereby weeding out unsatisfactory teachers before they obtain permanent job security. And Richard Murnane and colleagues (Murnane et. al, 1991) have pointed out the need for schools to do a better job of teacher recruiting. Neither of these ideas, however, addresses the problem of undue job protection for teachers who have acquired tenure.

Ultimately, to restore the proper balance with regard to removing misbehaving teachers, two things must be done. First, discharge procedures must cease allowing accused teachers to participate in the choice of the hearing officers and arbitrators who preside in these cases. An accused teacher is entitled to a fair tribunal, of course, but that tribunal should be imbued with strong community values—values that recognize the importance of maintaining safe, secure, and moral learning environments.

Second, teacher dismissal proceedings must become less time-consuming, expensive, and complex. It should not take two years or longer to bring these cases to resolution, and it should not require $200,000 or more in expenditures to establish a teacher's unsuitability in the classroom.

Many things can be done, of course, to streamline the administrative procedures for disciplining teachers and to make them less expensive.

Ultimately, however, the fundamental flaws in our teacher discipline processes are not procedural problems. The primary reason that teacher dismissal proceedings take so long and are so expensive is not because they are procedurally complex; rather, it is because educators have no commonly shared values about what constitutes proper grounds for dismissing a teacher.

The Sunnyvale case and the Flatbush case illustrate this point. In both cases, the central facts were not in dispute. Both men had been convicted of criminal offenses. Time and money were not expended to prove the misconduct; rather, battle was joined over whether the misconduct constituted grounds for dismissal.

In most teacher dismissal cases, this battle is fought between school boards and teachers' unions. School boards commonly take the view that teachers are role models in the community who should be held to high standards of morality. Teachers' unions usually take the view that no misconduct constitutes grounds for dismissal unless it can be shown that the misbehavior adversely affects the classroom environment in a tangible way.

For school reform to become a reality, school boards and teachers associations must develop common values about who should be permitted to teach children and what kind of conduct constitutes an irremediable breach of public trust. These values should be humane, recognizing that dedicated teachers sometimes make mistakes. On the other hand, teachers' organizations should acknowledge that certain behavior by its very nature demonstrates unfitness to teach.

At a minimum, teachers' unions and school boards should be able to agree that teachers who are dishonest, who violate drug laws or use illegal drugs, who disregard children's safety, or who physically or sexually abuse school children should be removed from the classroom. No one other than the perpetrators benefit from protracted legal battles about whether such people should retain their jobs.

Ideally, school boards and teachers organizations would be partners, rather than adversaries, when the competency or morality of a teacher is at issue. Indeed, we might expect school boards and teachers unions to share responsibility for identifying and removing incompetent, immoral, or poorly performing teachers.

In a few districts, school boards and teachers groups are working together in this area. In Toledo, for example, union leaders and administrators share responsibility for identifying substandard teachers and providing remediation, and in Cincinnati, a peer assistance and appraisal program involves teachers in evaluating and assisting poorly-performing tenured teachers (Kerchner & Koppich, 1993).

These districts and local unions are headed in the right direction. Unfortunately, in many, and perhaps most districts, school boards and unions are bitter adversaries in personnel matters. Ultimately, for this pattern to change, school boards and unions must modify the industrial model of labor relations, a model that assumes school boards and unions have fundamentally different interests in the workplace. Any new model that is created must be one that recognizes that teachers, administrators, and school board members have common interests when it comes to ensuring that only dedicated and moral educators are allowed to work in the public schools.

CONCLUSION

Schools can be great places for adults — annual raises, good health insurance, and job protection so good that even a teacher who falsely reports a bomb in a public school can escape the consequences of his actions. But some public schools, especially those in the inner cities, can be very uncongenial places for students, and a blizzard of school reform legislation has not done much to change that fact.

Job protection for grownups may be one reason our school reform efforts have not been more successful. If the Flatbush teacher and the Sunnyvale teacher can retain their positions, then surely the incompetent teacher, the surly teacher, and the merely indifferent teacher are completely secure in their jobs. In school districts where that is the case, site-based management, shared decision making, and teacher empowerment initiatives are not likely to change the school environment.

For school reform to become a reality, we must view teachers' job protection rights in a different light. First, we must ensure that the tribunals who make decisions about teacher discipline are not only fair and humane, but that they are imbued with community values about what constitutes minimally acceptable behavior.

Second, to achieve school reform, the various interest groups in public education must develop common values about who should be permitted to teach children. If this were to happen, school districts and teachers' unions could become partners, not adversaries, when evaluating teacher competency.

Finally, for American schools to improve, the adults who work in them must acknowledge that their job rights involve much more than their own self-interests. Educators must accept the proposition that a child's right to be taught by a moral, competent, and dedicated teacher is more important than a school employee's entitlement to a job.

REFERENCES

Annie E. Casey Foundation (1994). *Kids count data book*. Baltimore, MD: author.

Bassett Unified School District v. Commission on Professional Competence, 274 Cal. Rptr. 865 (Cal. App. 1988).

Bernard v. Avoyelles Parish School Board, 640 So.2d 321 (La.App. 1994).

Board of Education of Sunnyvale Elementary School District v. Commission on Professional Competence, 162 Cal. Rptr. 590 (Cal. Ct. App. 1980).

Bridges, E. M. (1988). Coping with incompetent teachers. In L. H. Golubchick and B. Persky (Eds.), Urban, social, and educational issues (pp. 158 – 161). Garden City Park, NY: Avery Publishing Group.

Clune, W. H. (1993). Systematic educational policy: A conceptual framework. In S. H. Fuhrman (Ed.), *Designing coherent educational policy: Improving the system* (pp. 125 – 140). San Francisco: Jossey-Bass.

Condon, T. (1993, March 28). Arrest leaves questions, but no answers. *Hartford (Connecticut) Courant,* p. b1.

Cortines, R. C. and Stancik, E. F. (1994). *Final report of the Joint Commission of the Chancellor and the special commissioner for the prevention of child sexual abuse.* New York, NY: New York City Board of Education.

Dillon, S. (1994, June 28). Teachers and tenure: Rights v. discipline. *The New York Times,* Section A, p. 1.

Erwin, K. (1994, September 24). Student reports affair 14 years later. *Baton Rouge Advocate.*

Finch, M. and Nagel, T. W. (1984). Collective bargaining in the public schools: Reassessing labor policy in an era of reform, *Wisconsin Law Review,* pp. 1573 – 1670.

Fossey, R. and Merseth, K. (1991). Anchorage School District. Harvard Graduate School of Education, teaching case.

Frahm, R. (1994, July 31). Teacher's dismissal is a test for all: Ridgefield case highlights process under tenure law. *Hartford Courant,* p. A1.

Goldberg, N. (1994, July 2). They're outta here; Legislature OKs bill to remove bad teachers. *Newsday.*

Howe, P. J. (1993, June 19). Weld puts lukewarm pen to education reform bill. *Boston Globe,* Metro/Regional sec., p. 10.

J. N. v. Bellingham School District No. 501, 871 P.2d 1106 (Wash. Ct. App. 1994).

Johnson, S. M. (1978). The case of Edna Wiley. Harvard Graduate School of Education, teaching case.

Kerchner, C. T. and Koppich, J. E. (1993). *A union of professionals: Labor relations and educational reform.* New York: Teachers College Press.

Maxcy, S. J. and Maxcy, D. O. (1993). Educational reform in Louisiana. *International Journal of Educational Reform* 2:236–241.

Murnane, R., Singer, J., Willett, J., Kemple, J. and Olsen, R. (1991). *Who will teach? Policies that matter.* Cambridge, MA: Harvard University Press.

Myers, D. (1994, August 22). 99% of teachers pass evaluations. *Baton Rouge Advocate.*

Nisbet, R. (1974). *The sociology of Emile Durkheim.* New York: Oxford University Press.

Renfroe v. Green, 626 P.2d 1068 (Alaska 1980).

Riverview School District v. Riverview Education Association, 639 A.2d 974 (Pa. Cmwth Ct. 1994).

Schmidt, P. (1994, September 28). Phila. leaders join call for overhaul of schools. *Education Week,* p. 3.

Shanker, A. (1992). The crisis in education and the limits of the traditional model of schooling. In J. J. Lane and E. G. Epps (Eds.), *Restructuring the schools: Problems and prospects* (pp. 3–14). Berkeley, CA: McCutchan.

Stein, N. D. (1993, December). Sexual harassment in schools, administrators must break the casual approach to objectionable behavior. *Administrator,* pp. 14–21.

Timar, T. and Kirp, D. (1988). *Managing educational excellence.* Philadelphia: Falmer Press.

Wilson, S. F. (1992). *Reinventing the schools: A radical plan for Boston.* Boston: Pioneer Institute.

CHAPTER 7

Remembering Jane and John Doe: Our Inexcusable Failure to Stop Sexual Abuse in Schools

> *The worst sin towards our fellow creatures is not to hate them, but to be indifferent to them: that is the essence of inhumanity.*
> —George Bernard Shaw, *The Devil's Disciple*

In May 1995, a security guard at a Washington, D.C. junior high school was sentenced to prison for sexually molesting two school children (Miller, 1995). Although the guard had been employed by the district since 1987, the school district had not conducted a criminal background check on him until 1993. That check turned up four arrests and a conviction for illegal possession of a firearm. Nevertheless, nothing was done with this information, and the guard continued to work for the district until after he was arrested for sexual abuse.

In the wake of this tragic incident, an audit was conducted of District of Columbia hiring practices. Auditors found that school officials had hired thousands of people who had been arrested or convicted of crimes. Among the auditors' discoveries was the fact that about a quarter of the district's 211 security workers had arrest or conviction records. Over a fifteen-month period ending in December 1994, the school district had hired 114 people with criminal backgrounds, about 6% of all its new employees (Strauss, 1995). More than fifty of these persons had been hired as teachers or substitute teachers.

Ironically, the District of Columbia's sloppy hiring practices persisted during a period of significant school reform. Indeed, the school where the offending security guard was employed had been named as one of forty-two District of Columbia schools selected to participate in a school-based management program (Leonhardt, 1994). This tragedy illustrates the fact that education reform initiatives, no matter how innovative, cannot achieve their full potential in schools where children are not safe. Reform efforts directed at curriculum changes, education funding, or school governance, but which neglect children's physical security, make false promises of school improvement.

Unfortunately, children are not as safe as they should be from sexual abuse in schools. Although it is impossible to determine exactly how much abuse occurs in school environments, recent studies show that it is not rare. In 1993, the American Association of University Women published a survey that reported that 25 percent of females in grades 8 through 11 and 10 percent of the males in that age group had been sexually harassed in some way at school by an adult. An earlier study found that a majority of children were sexually harassed at one time or another by an adult at school during some point in their elementary or secondary education (Wishnietsky, 1991).

HOW ABUSE HAPPENS

Little research has been done on sexual abuse in the schools, and school districts are reluctant to release details of these incidents. Nevertheless, some sexual abuse victims have sued the school districts that employed the perpetrators. Often brought in the name of ''Jane Doe'' or ''John Doe'' to preserve the victim's privacy, these cases tell us much about how schools become settings for child abuse.

First, as court cases illustrate, sexual abuse in schools usually involves multiple incidents and multiple victims. For example:

- In a Tennessee case, several high school girls charged that they were sexually abused by a teacher in a series of incidents stretching over a period of three years (*Jane Doe v. Coffee County Board of Education*, 1992).
- In Alabama, four elementary-school boys, ranging in ages from eight to eleven, accused a teacher of molesting them for a year or more. The alleged incidents occurred in the classroom, on school outings, and in the teacher's home (*John Does 1, 2, 3, and 4 v. Covington County School Board*, 1995).

• In a Louisiana school district, a band director was convicted of sexually molesting two fourteen-year-old female band students on separate occasions during the same school year. One girl was taken out of her home economics class and molested in the school band room. The other girl was molested in the school library during band practice (*State v. Moses,* 1993).

Research studies confirm that sexual molestation in the schools often involves several victims and multiple incidents. In a 1991 article, Professor Gail Sorenson surveyed court cases involving child abuse in the schools over a four-year period. Out of thirty-seven cases, twenty involved multiple victims, and thirty described multiple acts of abuse against the same individual. A federal probe of suspected child abuse at Indian reservation schools, described in a journal article, reported that one teacher avoided detection for eighteen years before he was arrested. Another arrested teacher was found to have kept records of his sexual activities with 142 Indian children (Schafer & McIlwaine, 1992).

In addition, court cases tell us that child abuse in schools is often a crime of opportunity. Court records show that certain categories of school employees figure prominently in cases of sexual abuse and harassment: male coaches, band directors, and extracurricular advisors. These adults tend to be held in high regard by students and have more opportunities to have one-on-one contact with them—often in private settings—than do other teachers. Coaches and band directors usually have access to isolated settings such as training and dressing rooms, empty gyms, and band practice rooms. Sexual assaults often take place in these settings.

Studies also show that children with physical and mental disabilities and behavioral disorders may be particularly vulnerable to sexual abuse (Pettis & Hughes, 1985). Several court cases involve accusations that the abuse took place while such students were being transported to or from school (*Musgrave v. Lopez,* 1993; *Roe v. Lawn,* 1993).

IGNORANCE AND INDIFFERENCE TOWARD SEXUAL ABUSE IN SCHOOLS

Ignorance is one reason educators have not been as successful as they could be in stopping child abuse in the schools. Several studies have shown that educators do not fully understand the child abuse reporting laws and that they are poorly trained in detecting child abuse (Shoop & Firestone, 1988; Lombard et al., 1986). McIntyre (1990) found that teachers were particularly ignorant of the signs of sexual abuse. Only 4 percent said they were very aware of signs of sexual abuse, 17 percent reported that they could recognize signs of sexual abuse if they were obvious, and an astonishing 75 percent reported that they could not recognize signs of sexual abuse at any point. McIntyre's study also reported that more than half the teachers surveyed said that they had never had an abused or neglected child in their classroom despite the fact that a majority of the nation's abused children are in pubic school classrooms on any given school day.

A recent report on sexual abuse investigations in the New York City Public Schools illustrates how ineffective unskilled school leaders can sometimes be when confronted with accusations of sexual misconduct against a school employee. A panel of sixty child-welfare advocates, mental health experts, educators, and union representatives found that schools in New York City often mishandled complaints of child sexual abuse in ways that traumatized victims and allowed abusers to continue working with children (New York City Board of Education, 1994).

The panel examined 110 substantiated cases of sexual abuse that were handled by the school system's special commission of investigations. This examination revealed that many well-meaning district employees would conduct their own inquiries prior to complying with the child abuse reporting laws and that these inquiries often jeopardized subsequent investigations or needlessly damaged some employees' reputations and careers. The panel also found that principals sometimes did not report abusers promptly or at all, particularly when they feared a report would damage their school's reputation (New York City Board of Education, 1994).

This widespread ignorance about child abuse is puzzling, given the critical role that educators have been given to detect and report child abuse and neglect. All fifty states require teachers and school administrators to report their suspicions of child abuse to child-welfare authorities, and all states impose significant civil or criminal penalties against educators who knowingly fail to make these reports (Myers, 1986). Nevertheless, most educators receive no training about their child abuse reporting obligations in their undergraduate teacher training courses and no inservice training after they begin their teaching careers.

Likewise, graduate-level courses for school administrators rarely touch on the topic of child abuse.

Ignorance is not the only reason that child abuse occurs in our pubic schools. Unfortunately, in some public schools, there is a culture of indifference concerning this kind of misbehavior. Co-workers may be aware of a school employee's propensity for sexual exploitation without taking any action. In fact, many court cases describe repeated incidents of sexual molestation taking place on school property during the school day. It seems unlikely that this kind of misbehavior could take place for an extended period of time without an offender's colleagues becoming aware of it.

How could an educator stand by and do nothing when confronted with evidence that a child is being molested at school by a co-worker? Perhaps the best way to answer this question is to present a case study that illustrates how such things occur.

The following case study is extracted from a federal appeals court ruling in which a high school girl sued her school district for failing to protect her from a teacher's sexual advances. At the time the court's opinion was rendered, the girl's allegations had not been established as factually true. Rather, the court accepted them as true only for the purpose of determining whether her charges, if later proven, established the basis for a lawsuit. In our case study, the names of the principal parties and the school district itself have been disguised.

JANE DOE AND PINEVILLE SCHOOL DISTRICT: A CASE STUDY

John Jakes, a biology teacher and coach for more than twenty years, was employed by the Pineville School District from 1981 to 1987. As early as 1985, complaints about Coach Jakes and his fancy for female students reached the offices of the principal and the district's superintendent. Jakes made little effort to conceal his interest in his female students, often writing explicit love letters to them, allowing them to drive his truck, and physically touching them in an inappropriate manner. His romantic affections for a number of young girls was not a secret within the school.

In the fall of 1986, Jane Doe entered Pineville High School as a freshman. Coach Jakes quickly became enamored with her to the point of obsession. He would give her high grades without requiring her to do any work. He would take her and other high school girls to lunch away from school during the school day, and he occasionally bought alcoholic beverages for Jane and other girls. With all this attention lavished on her, it was not surprising when Jane Doe developed a "crush" on Coach Jakes.

By late fall, Jakes was taking Doe into the field house and the laboratory room adjacent to the biology classroom, where kissing and touching escalated to heavy petting and undressing. In January 1987, after Jakes had taken Doe to a rock concert, he bought her alcoholic beverages and took her back to the field house and suggested that they have sexual intercourse. She refused.

On Valentine's Day, Coach Jakes gave Jane Doe a Valentine that read, "To my most favorite, prettiest, nicest sweetheart in the world! Please don't change cause I need you. I'm in love with you. Forever—for real—I love you." Beth, Jane Doe's friend and classmate, found the Valentine in Jane Doe's purse and took it to the principal, Delbert Hickle. Beth told Hickle she suspected that Jakes was sexually involved with Jane Doe. Hickle acknowledged that he was aware of rumors concerning Coach Jakes and Jane Doe, but he indicated that Jakes just had a way of flirting with girls. Hickle then transferred Beth, not Doe, out of Jakes's class and did not investigate the matter further. He did not contact Jakes about the Valentine or the rumors.

After the Valentine's Day Dance, Jane Doe spent the night at Jakes's house. Doe and Jakes's daughter had become friends, but it was Jakes who had invited Doe to spend the night. While at the house, Jakes again suggested sexual intercourse, but again, Doe refused. Over the course of the next two months, Doe spent several nights at Jakes's home. Each time, Jakes would try to convince Doe to have sexual intercourse with him, and each time she refused.

By this time, Jakes's relationship with Jane Doe was becoming less and less of a secret. One week after the Valentine's Day Dance, the superintendent, Homer Dimler, learned from another school administrator that Jakes was behaving "unprofessionally" with Doe. The superintendent, principal Hickle, and the athletic director spoke to Jakes about these allegations. The athletic director had spoken to Jakes before about allegations of sexual misconduct with students. The athletic director informed Hickle about these discussions as they took place. Hickle had informed Dimler about several of the reports concerning Jakes.

In early spring 1987, Jane Doe gave in to Jakes's pressure and had sexual intercourse with him. Jane Doe said later in a deposition that she gave in to Jakes because she was tired of Jakes's pressure. She sensed that Jakes was getting angry with her for refusing his advances, and she was afraid of losing his friendship. Doe was fifteen years old, and Jakes was her first sexual partner.

Over the next several months, Jakes and Jane Doe had sexual intercourse and oral sex both on and off the school grounds. Their relationship (although perhaps not the full extent of it) had become common knowledge within the Pineville High School Community of students, parents, and faculty. During this time, Doe was reluctant to refuse Jakes's sexual advances for fear of alienating him.

In June 1987, Jakes took Jane Doe and some other girls to a festival where he provided them with alcoholic beverages. One girl became drunk, and Jakes's wife became angry because Jakes danced with Jane Doe. Jakes later took Doe into a field where they had sexual intercourse. After that, Jakes took Doe, his daughter, and the intoxicated girl back to his home, where he again had sexual intercourse with Doe.

Two concerned parents who witnessed some of Jakes's behavior at the festival reported it to Superintendent Dimler. They also stated that Jakes exhibited favoritism toward female students in his classes. Superintendent Dimler never contacted Doe's parents, nor did he contact Jakes or investigate the parents' complaints.

In July 1987, Jane Doe's parents discovered photographs of Jakes among Doe's possessions. The pictures had handwritten inscriptions on them, such as, ''Please don't ever change and don't leave me. I want to be close always—I love you—Coach Jakes.'' Doe's parents immediately brought the photographs to Superintendent Dimler. Dimler admitted to Doe's parents that he was aware of rumors concerning Coach Jakes. He promised to convene a meeting of all concerned parties. The meeting never took place.

Dimler did, however, meet with Jane Doe. When questioned at the meeting, Doe suggested that the note on the photograph was a friendly gesture. She explicitly denied having sexual intercourse with Jakes. Principal Hickle warned Jakes that he would be fired if it were determined that Jakes had an inappropriate relationship with Doe. After talking with Jakes and Doe, Hickle took no further action. Dimler told Doe that he would go with her to the police if such action were warranted, but he too investigated the matter no further.

The sexual liaison between Jakes and Doe ceased for the remainder of the summer. But when classes began in the fall, Jakes recommenced his pursuit of Doe. In October 1987, Doe's mother found love letters from Jakes. Doe's parents contacted their family attorney, who agreed to meet with Doe. At the meeting, she confessed her sexual involvement with Jakes. The attorney immediately reported this revelation to Superintendent Dimler. Coincidentally, another female student contacted Dimler on the same day, reporting that Jakes had made sexual advances toward her.

This time, school authorities acted. Jakes was suspended without pay. He later resigned and pled guilty to criminal charges stemming from sexual activity with Jane Doe.

"PASSING THE TRASH": COVERING UP EVIDENCE OF CHILD ABUSE

In Jane Doe's case, the Pineville school authorities eventually took action against an abusive teacher, although their reaction time was slow. In the end, Jakes was convicted of criminal charges. Unfortunately, in some instances, school officials try to sweep child abuse allegations "under the rug," without ever notifying teacher-licensing authorities or the police. In order to save the expense of dismissal proceedings, districts often induce an accused teacher to resign by offering him a reference letter in return for waiving the right to a dismissal hearing (Fossey, 1990). Typically, the teacher finds a job in another district, and the truth or falsity of the allegation against him are never determined.

This practice of disposing of problem teachers, sometimes referred to as "passing the trash," can be dangerous to children. As Nan Stein (1993) pointed out, the practice can lead to the creation of "mobile molesters," renegade teachers who molest children in several communities as they move from school district to school district.

INADEQUATE LEGAL REMEDIES FOR THE VICTIMS OF SEXUAL ABUSE

One sure way of making school authorities more vigilant in preventing child abuse by school employees would be to impose substantial legal penalties when abuse occurs. School districts would almost certainly do a better job in this area if they knew they could be forced to pay damages to a family whose child was molested while in the school's care.

So far, however, the courts have not provided a sure remedy for children who are sexually abused by school employees. In case after case, school children and their families have sued school districts for their injuries, only to have their cases thrown out of court.

In many jurisdictions, state immunity laws, which protect school boards and administrators from negligence suits, bar child abuse victims from recovering damages from school districts. In states that have such laws, children cannot seek damages from school districts no matter how negligent school officials have been. Of course, the child can still sue the actual abuser, but in most cases, such a suit would be futile because the perpetrator is penniless and in jail.

Even in states that permit negligence suits against school districts, school authorities can usually rely on very effective legal defenses to avoid liability. Several state courts have ruled that school employees act outside the scope of their employment when they commit a sexual assault, and thus school districts are not accountable (*Bozarth v. Harper Creek Board of Education*, 1980; *Boykin v. District of Columbia*, 1984).

Interestingly enough, courts are sometimes more willing to fashion a remedy when a government employee assaults an adult than when the victim is a child (Fossey & DeMitchell, 1995). The California Supreme Court ruled that the Los Angeles police department was liable when a police officer raped a woman motorist who had been stopped for a traffic violation (*Mary M. v. City of Los Angeles*, 1991); but the same court ruled that the Oakland school district was not responsible when a teacher sexually assaulted a school child (*John R. v. Oakland Unified School District*, 1989).

Finding state courts inhospitable, child abuse victims and their families have begun suing in federal court. A federal appellate court ruled, in *Stoneking v. Bradford Area School District* (1989), that a public school principal could be held liable for damages in a case where a former high school student charged that she had been sexually exploited by a school band director for three years and that the principal was aware of the accusations but failed to investigate them.

In *Jane Doe v. Taylor (Texas) Independent School District* (1994), the Fifth Circuit Court of Appeals issued a similar ruling. In that case, a student claimed that the principal failed to protect her from a teacher's sexual advances in spite of reports to the principal about the teacher's misconduct from the school librarian, a counselor, two community members, and at least one student.

Stoneking and *Jane Doe v. Taylor ISD* sparked concern among teachers and school administrators when they first appeared. Educators feared the rulings would increase their exposure to damages if a school child was assaulted by a school employee. It now seems clear, however, that the federal courts are not as hospitable to child abuse victims as some commentators first thought. Both cases were decided on the principle that a child has a constitutional right to bodily integrity that is violated when she is sexually assaulted by a school employee. School districts and other employees cannot be held liable for the injuries, however, unless the child can show that they acted with deliberate indifference to her constitutional rights.

Federal courts have made it clear that, for the purposes of imposing liability on school districts, "deliberate indifference" amounts to more than mere negligence. The child must show that there is a level of indifference that amounts almost to callousness about her plight. Thus, in a Texas case, a court ruled that school officials had not violated the constitutional rights of a child who had been sexually molested by a teacher, in spite of the fact that school officials had received an earlier complaint about the teacher and had simply transferred him to another school (*Gonzalez v. Ysleta Independent School District*, 1993).

In the late 1980s, a line of cases emerged in which child abuse victims argued that school officials had an affirmative constitutional duty to protect them from sexual assaults. They reasoned that children, like prisoners and mental patients, are in a custodial relationship with the state and that this relationship imposes an affirmative duty on school officials to protect children from harm. This argument has been almost universally rejected by the federal courts, sometimes rather callously (Fossey, 1994). "The analogy of a school yard to a prison may be a popular one for school-age children," one federal court observed, "but we cannot recognize constitutional duties on a child's lament" (*J. O. v. Alton Community Unit School District 11*, 1990).

SIGNS OF CHANGE IN THE COURTS

Although the courts have not been as welcoming to child abuse victims as they should be, there are some hopeful signs of change. In *Leija v. Canutillo Independent School District* (1995), a federal court ruled that a Texas school district was vicariously liable for a teacher's sexual abuse of a student, without regard to whether district officials had been negligent. The decision was based on Title IX of the Education Amendments of 1973, a federal law that prohibits sex discrimination in schools that receive federal funds.

Acknowledging the financial impact of its ruling on the school district, the *Leija* court limited the child's damages to the reasonable cost of treatment—medical, counseling, and special education expenses. According to the court, limiting damages in this way would provide money for services which were most likely to heal the child, but the damages would not be so great that the district's ability to serve other students would be impaired (DeMitchell & Fossey, 1996).

The U.S. Supreme Court had previously ruled that school districts could be sued under Title IX when a teacher molests a school child (*Franklin v. Gwinnett County Public Schools,* 1992), but the standards for assessing liability were not made clear in the Supreme Court decision. The recent *Leija* decision adopts the view that a child-molesting employee is the school district's agent, even when he is abusing a child. Thus, the school district must pay for the injuries its agent causes.

CONCLUSION

A central purpose of law is to protect the weak from the strong and to compensate victims for injuries caused by carelessness and neglect. Unfortunately, when confronted by child abuse in the schools, courts often fail to fashion effective remedies. Consciously or unconsciously, indifferent educators know they run only a small risk of being personally penalized if a child is raped or molested while in their care.

In an ideal world, teachers and school administrators would keep children safe, regardless of whether they could be held liable for a child's injuries. But this is not an ideal world, and far too many educators are indifferent to child abuse that takes place around them. To ensure their diligence, they must face significant sanctions if a child is abused while in their care.

The following remedies are needed: First, school districts should pay damages every time a child is sexually abused by a school employee, regardless of whether the child can prove negligence on the part of school authorities. The rationale of the *Leija* court is a sensible approach to making the victim whole. Currently, Title IX holds the most promise for making this principle a general rule of law. To prevent schools from being rendered insolvent by large claims, damages should be limited to reasonable medical, counseling, and special education expenses.

Second, educators who fail to report suspected child abuse by a coworker should be personally liable in damages, a principle that some, but not all, courts have adopted. As with school districts, an individual educator's liability should be limited to the cost of the child's treatment.

Third, school districts that "pass the trash," by allowing known child abusers to obtain work in other districts should pay damages for their callousness, as should the administrators and school board members who participate in such shell games. Revocation or suspension of administrative credentials should be considered for administrators who knowingly give molesters positive letters of recommendation.

These may seem like harsh remedies, but unfortunately they are necessary to shake educators out of their apathy about sexual abuse in the schools. Indeed, expanding schools' liability for their employees' sexual molestation is justified even if it diverts financial resources away from school reform initiatives. In the final analysis, a child's physical and psychological integrity is more basic than any school reform. In schools where educators are indifferent to children's safety, school reform — regardless of the strategy — will not be successful. Unless we remember this simple fact, we will have schools that are neither reformed nor safe.

REFERENCES

American Association of University Women. (1993). *Hostile hallways: The AAUW survey on sexual harassment in America's Schools*. Washington, D.C.: AAUW Educational Foundation.

Boykin v. District of Columbia, 484 A.2d 560 (D.C. App. 1984).

Bozarth v. Harper Creek Board of Education, 288 N.W.2d 424 (Mich. Ct. App. 1980).

DeMitchell, T. A. and Fossey, R. (1996). Strict liability under Title IX for employee sexual abuse of students: *Leija v. Canutillo Independent School District. International Journal of Educational Reform* 5: 107–114.

Fossey, R. (1990). Confidential settlement agreements between school districts and teachers accused of child abuse: Issues of law and ethics. *Education Law Reporter* 63:1–10.

Fossey, R. (1994). Law, trauma, and sexual abuse in the schools: Why can't children protect themselves? *Education Law Reporter* 91:443–454.

Fossey, R. and DeMitchell, T. A. (1995, April 21). "Let the master respond": Should schools be strictly liable when employees sexually abuse children? *American*

Educational Research Association Annual Meeting, San Francisco, California. ERIC document No. EA 027043.

Franklin v. Gwinnett County Public Schools, 506 U.S. 60 (1992).

Gonzalez v. Ysleta Independent School District, 996 F.2d. 745 (5th Cir. 1993).

J. O. v. Alton Community Unit School District 11, 909 F.2d 267 (7th Cir. 1990).

Jane Doe v. Coffee County Bd. of Education., 852 S.W.2d 899 (Tenn. Ct. App. 1992).

Jane Doe v. Taylor Independent School District, 15 F.3d 443 (5th Cir. 1994).

John Does 1, 2, 3, and 4 v. Covington County School Board, 884 F.Supp. 462 (M.D. Ala. 1995).

John R. v. Oakland Unified School District, 448 Cal. 3d 438 (1989).

Leija v. Canutillo Independent School District, 887 F.Supp. 947 (W.D. Tex. 1995).

Leonhardt, D. (1994, June 16). 42 City schools given more power to improve; some staffs get right to develop curriculum. *Washington Post,* p. J3.

Lombard, F. K., Michalka, M. J., and Pearlman, T. A. (1986). Identifying the abused child: A study of reporting practices of teachers. *University of Detroit Law Review* 63:657−676.

Mary M. v. City of Los Angeles, 814 P.2d 1341, 1343 (Cal. 1991).

McIntyre, T. (1990). The teacher's role in cases of suspected child abuse. *Education and Urban Society* 22:300−306.

Miller, B. (1995, May 12). School guard is sentenced for molesting D.C. youths; arrest led to systemwide check of employees. *Washington Post,* p. C03.

Musgrave v. Lopez, 861 S.W.2d 262 (Tex. Ct. App. 1993).

Myers, J. (1986). A survey of child abuse reporting laws. *Journal of Juvenile Law* 10: 1−72.

New York City Board of Education (1994, October). *Final Report of the Joint Commission of the Chancellor and Special Commissioner for the Prevention of Child Sexual Abuse.*

Pettis, K. W. and Hughes, R. D. (1985). Sexual victimization of children: Implications for educators. *Behavioral Disorders* 10:175−182.

Roe v. Lawn, 615 N.E.2d 944 (Mass. Ct. App. 1993).

Schafer, J. R. and McIlwaine, B. D. (1992). Investigating child sexual abuse in the American Indian community. *American Indian Quarterly* 16:157−167.

Shoop, R. J. and Firestone, L. M. (1988). Mandatory reporting of suspected child abuse: Do teachers obey the law? *Education Law Reporter* 46:1115−1122.

Sorenson, G. P. (1991). Sexual abuse in schools: Reported cases from 1987−1990. *Educational Administration Quarterly* 27:460−480.

State v. Moses, 615 So.2d 1030 (La. Ct. App. 1993).

Stein, N. D. (1993, January). Sexual harassment in schools, administrators must break the casual approach to objectionable behavior. *Administrator,* pp. 14−19.

Stoneking v. Bradford Area School District, 882 F.2d 720 (3rd Cir. 1989), cert. denied, 493 U.S. 1044 (1990).

Strauss, V. (1995, April 14). Board to urge schools to fire workers with serious records. *Washington Post,* p. C1.

Wishnietsky, Dan H. (1991). Reported and unreported teacher-student sexual harassment. *Journal of Educational Research* 3:164−169.

PART FOUR

LITIGATION AND LEGISLATION: IN DUBIOUS BATTLE FOR REFORM

CHAPTER 8

Opposition Forces and Education Reform: Will Charter Schools Succeed?**

> *Charter schools are fine so long as school boards are driving the bus.*
> —Billy Walker, Executive Director, Texas Association of
> School Boards (Porterfield, 1994, p. A1)

Searching for a cure to the problems of our country's public schools has become a national obsession. For the past three decades, a number of initiatives have been discussed, debated, and adopted. The 1970s brought standardized testing, minimum standards, and many new "programs" as the medicines of choice. Reform efforts in the 1980s included increased graduation requirements, career ladders or merit pay programs for teachers, site-based decision making, and additional state dollars. The early 1990s have focused on higher academic standards for students, a push for vouchers, and decentralization. To date, none of these initiatives has provided an acceptable "cure" for the nation's public schools. Appropriate and adequate means to seriously change the system—not just improve slightly—have not existed. As a nation, we continue to be disappointed with standardized test scores, drop-out rates, and tests that compare students from the United States with students from other countries.

Accompanying each proposed cure is the expectation that the next proposal will, if implemented, systemically reform public education.

**This chapter was authored by Louann A. Bierlein and Mark Bateman.

Parents, educators, and policy makers begin to trumpet the new reform as a certain cure. However, expectations are often unrealistic, ultimately leading to disappointment. Too often, when a reform is examined in retrospect, it is found that the reform concept was not sound, or if originally sound, the reform was derailed or fundamentally undermined by "status quo" forces of the system.

CHARTER SCHOOLS: THE NEWEST CURE

The concept of charter schools is the latest up and coming cure. Viewed as a means to both empower those within the system to change and to unleash internal and external competitive forces, the charter school concept has caught the attention of many.

Beginning with Minnesota in 1991, twenty-five states and the District of Columbia have enacted some type of charter school legislation (as of October 1996). Many other states have considered and will continue to consider such legislation. Although few individuals believe charter schools are a panacea— as was often the case for previous reforms—expectations are high that these schools will make a difference. Indeed, former Secretary of Education Terrel Bell (1995) recently wrote that "the charter-school idea has emerged as possibly the most promising innovation [yet]" (p. 40).

The big question is whether the charter school concept is powerful enough medicine to become meaningful reform or whether it will become just another watered down cure. We contend that it is too early to determine if charter schools will succeed, but we are not overly optimistic. Our opinion is based on the belief that, although charter schools have already accomplished a great deal and hold promise for shaking up the current system, many status quo groups are finding charter schools a bitter pill to swallow. Powerful interests have mobilized to defeat this reform effort.

This chapter examines the concept of charter schools, their appeal to reformers, and the resistance to their implementation. Specifically, the conceptual underpinnings of charter schools will be identified, as will the forces impeding the long-term success of the charter school movement.

CHARTER SCHOOLS: THE CONCEPT AND THE APPEAL

Ideally, a charter school is a public entity that is conceptualized, organized, and eventually operated by teachers, parents, and others from the public or private sector (Bierlein & Mulholland, 1994). The school operates under a charter (or contract) that has been negotiated between the school's organizers and a sponsor (such as a local school board, a state board of education, or university) that oversees the provisions of the charter. The charter itself describes the school's instructional plan, specific educational outcomes and measures, and the management and financial plan for the school. Charter schools may be formed using an entire school's existing personnel and facilities, a portion of such a school (called a school-within-a-school), or a completely new entity with its own facilities and staff.

Once a charter is granted, the school becomes an independent legal entity with the ability to hire and fire, sue and be sued, award contracts for outside services, and control its finances. Charter schools are "public" in the sense that they receive state funding, are nonsectarian, and are prohibited from being selective in student admission or charging tuition. They are also a school of choice for teachers, students, and parents; if the school fails to attract these individuals or violates any terms of its charter, it goes out of business. Charter schools are freed from most state laws and local board policies (except for health, safety, civil rights, fiscal and pupil accountability, etc.) and are granted full authority over public funding that follows students. In exchange for freedom from regulations, charter schools agree to be accountable for improved student outcomes.

Overall, there are many elements that make the creation of charter schools an appealing reform concept. Charter schools focus on results, not inputs; they also create more educational choices for teachers, parents, and students; they allow school-site personnel and parents to make administrative and instructional decisions and hold them legally liable for them; and they also create a more market-driven educational system (Mulholland & Bierlein, 1995). They also force questioning of many conventional public school management, instructional, and accountability practices: Who says that only local school boards should have the right to govern schools? Why can't school personnel and parents be given full control over all funds associated with their student count, including salaries? Hasn't the time come when educators, as part of a collective school entity, should be expected to demonstrate progress or face losing their jobs?

The ultimate appeal of charter schools, however, is that they are public entities, incorporating perhaps the best of the current public school world (e.g., protection for students and public funds) and the best of the private school world (e.g., competition, full site control). They also involve two types of accountability not found in combination in either world – they must both attract students *and* demonstrate specific results to some public entity or go out of business. However, as state policy makers attempt to enact charter school laws, much of this charter school ''ideal'' fails to become reality.

SEVEN CRITICAL COMPONENTS

Although model charter school legislation is available, state policy makers face many constraints when attempting to translate the charter school concept into actual law. These constraints include the provisions of each state's constitution, school financing systems, tradition, and perhaps most critical of all, the political clout of various education groups. As a result, only a few states have come close to allowing the creation of an unlimited number of ''ideal'' charter schools (as described in the previous section). These states are considered to have ''stronger'' charter school laws, wherein such schools can be sponsored by entities other than local boards, are granted a great deal of financial and legal autonomy, and are automatically free from most state and local rules. Perhaps as a result, more charter school activity is occurring. For example, as of October 1996, nearly 374 charter schools had been approved in the six initial states with stronger charter school laws.

In states with ''weaker'' laws, charter schools are often no more than enhanced site-based decision-making experiments: schools must remain part of the school district, have limited control over budget and personnel matters, and seek waivers from regulations on a case-by-case basis. In the initial five weaker states, only twenty-nine schools had been approved as of July 1995. Caution is urged, therefore, in lumping various charter school laws into a single category. All charter school laws (and the resulting schools for that matter) are not created equally.

Table 8.1 summarizes the seven key components that are considered essential to creating charter schools capable of challenging status quo elements of the system and, ultimately, producing broader reform results. These essential components are discussed below, with examples provided to illustrate their impact on potential charter schools.

Component #1: *A charter school must be allowed to seek sponsorship*

TABLE 8.1 *Key components of "stronger" charter laws.*

"Stronger" Charter Laws	"Weaker" Charter-like Laws
1) Public entities other than local district boards (e.g., intermediate or state boards, higher education) can approve (or sponsor) the charter school, or there is a strong appeal process.	1) Only local school boards can approve the charter school.
2) Any individual or group can attempt to organize a charter proposal.	2) Only select groups, such as certified teachers, can attempt to organize a charter proposal.
3) Charter schools are automatically exempt from nearly all state laws and rules and local policies (except health, safety, civil rights, etc.).	3) Charter schools must seek waivers on a case-by-case basis.
4) Fiscal autonomy—Charter schools receive and have full control over all state, federal, and local funds generated by their student count (they may contract with the district or other outside entities for services).	4) Funds remain under the control of the local district, or the law requires that a certain percentage automatically remains with the district.
5) Legal autonomy—Charter employees are employees of the charter school (not the local district), with the charter board determining salary and contract provisions, or the charter (not the law) determines status of employees.	5) Charter employees remain employees of a local district, with salaries and contract provisions still determined by the district board (rather than charter board).
6) There are no (or very high) limits on the number of charter schools that can be formed within a given state.	6) There are very low limits on the number of allowable charter schools (when compared with the total schools within a given state).
7) Individuals other than certified teachers are allowed to teach at the charter school (w/out having to seek a waiver).	7) Only certified teachers are allowed to teach at the school.

from a public entity other than a local school board and/or be allowed to appeal a school board decision. School boards have historically been the sole providers of and primary decision makers for public education in their communities. They hold a monopoly over the public education industry and do not give up power willingly or easily. History also suggests that local boards are not known to be innovative or to push for sweeping changes. Political pressures on these board members often ensure a level of "sameness" across the district in the areas of curriculum, management, salaries, and benefits. It is essential, therefore, to provide charter school applicants with the ability to appeal an unfavorable local board decision to some higher authority or to bypass their local boards completely, going directly to an alternate sponsor (such as a state board or university).

An appeals process puts pressure on local boards to carefully consider charter proposals based on the soundness of the plan, while the availability of alternate sponsors forces local boards to compete for their students. For example, many local boards in Arizona began to actively solicit charter proposals in the hopes that groups would stay with them rather than go to one of two state boards authorized to grant charter approvals. In response to Massachusetts's charter law, where proposals go directly to the commissioner of education, the Boston Public Schools and its teachers union initiated their own process for creating charter schools.

Local school board associations have fought hard against having alternative charter school sponsors or an appeal process (as well as the whole charter school concept), yet, once in place, some local board members are seeing the potential of charter schools within their districts. In Colorado, the executive director of that state's association of school boards noted: "Make no mistake about it: Colorado's Association of School Boards opposed the bill creating charter schools. . . . [We] worked vigorously before and during the legislative session to shape charter schools into a bill that would be more acceptable to local school board members. When that did not happen, we worked just as vigorously to kill the bill" (Quinn, 1993, p. 2). He then goes on to note that charter schools may indeed be "viewed as an opportunity to do something new and creatively different" (p. 2).

Some local boards in Colorado have taken this message to heart and are actively chartering schools in their districts, while others continue to resist the concept. As of March 1995, a total of twenty-three charter applicants in Colorado had appealed the denial of their charter proposal to their state board. Of these, five were remanded back to the local board for reconsideration (Fitzgerald, 1995). One appealed to the state board a second time when its local board still refused to grant them a charter. These examples illustrate why an alternative sponsor and/or appeals process is a critical component of a strong charter school law.

Component #2: *Any individual or group should be allowed to develop and submit a charter school proposal.* Creative energies from outside the traditional public education system are necessary to support serious reform efforts. Limiting the creation of charter schools to those currently in the system (i.e., certified teachers and existing public schools) ensures that a large percentage of the population continues to be excluded. Indeed, groups such as Big Brothers/Big Sisters, YMCAs, and private corporations are implementing charter schools in states that allow this activity. Given the continued lack of resources and the growing needs of students, policies that allow and encourage "outsiders" to become an active part of the solution are important.

The idea of allowing outsiders to form charter schools has been challenged by many in education circles. Some have argued that religious groups will gain access to public funds, while others claim that those interested in profiteering will corrupt education. Indeed, a number of applicants have been turned down for these reasons. Arizona, for example, has refused to grant final charter approvals to a small percent of applicants based upon fingerprinting and financial background checks. Others have been refused because their proposed curriculum had religious connotations.

Although caution is warranted in opening the door too far, many creative partnerships and charter schools are in existence as a result of this openness. Examples include: the Skills for Tomorrow Charter School, a vocational/technical school in Minnesota being run with support from the Teamsters Union; the Boston Renaissance Charter School, which is being implemented through a partnership between the Horace Mann Foundation and the Edison Project; the Atlantis Charter School (Fall River, MA), developed by a communitywide collaboration involving leaders from the public and private sectors; and the U.S. Drug Enforcement Administration, which is currently developing a charter proposal for Detroit. Any risk associated with granting "outsiders" responsibility for public education appears small when compared to the energy and support being generated in those states allowing this essential charter school component.

Component #3: *Charter schools must automatically be exempt from most state laws, regulations, and local policies (except health, safety, civil rights, etc.).* Some charter school states require applicants to request waivers from specific laws, rules, or policies on a case-by-case basis, rather than granting them automatic blanket waivers. This weakens the charter school concept in a number of ways. First, these schools must start with all existing laws and policies in place and seek to remove those that are found to be barriers. This is of concern since it is always more difficult to remove an obstruction than to proceed with no obstruction in the first place.

Second, without blanket exemptions, charter schools will continue to have an excuse for failure: we can't do something because the state and/or district won't let us! Fuhrman and Elmore (1995) recently examined this issue as part of their study of state deregulation efforts (for public schools in general, not just charter schools). They concluded that, although a number of states had waiver provisions on the books, only modest impacts were visible as a result of these provisions. They noted that it was often not the actual regulations themselves that were barriers, but the lack of knowledge regarding a given regulation. It is simply easier to believe that something couldn't be done than to carefully check the provisions (which is almost impossible for school personnel to do anyway). The "liberation of 'no excuses' planning" was more important than freedom from an actual regulation (p. 13). To this end, the component of automatic exemptions is important, in that it immediately sets the stage for "no excuses" planning for charter schools.

Components #4 and #5: *Charter schools must have fiscal* and *legal autonomy.* In reference to fiscal autonomy, it is difficult, and perhaps unfair, to hold individuals or entities responsible for progress when they do not have full control over all resources. When charter laws require schools to negotiate over the amount of funding they will receive, the balance of power continues to reside with the local board. Providing full funding to successful charter school applicants minimizes the disputes that can arise from the negotiation process. Charter schools, in turn, can still subcontract back with their district for many of the services that district central offices provide.

Legal autonomy for charter schools is also essential. First, local boards should not be legally liable for the actions of the charter school. If charter schools gain full control over funding and decision making, then those within the school (including the charter board) should be fully responsible for their actions (i.e., they get sued, not the local school board). Second, by becoming a legal entity, a charter school takes on the responsibility for school employees. Education is a personnel intensive industry, and charter schools must therefore have ultimate control over salaries, evaluations, and employment terms. Clearly, these activities concern teacher unions; however, all teachers at charter schools are there because they want to be—these are schools of choice for students, parents, and teachers alike.

What can be accomplished with such legal and fiscal autonomy? The best example to date is Vaughn Next Century Learning Center, a charter school in the heart of Los Angeles. Under the leadership of a dynamic principal, the school ended the year with a $1.0 million surplus (out of an initial $4.6 million budget) during its first year as a charter school, after lowering class sizes and restoring a districtwide teacher pay cut (Y. Chan, personnel communication, April 10, 1995). These funds were used, in part, to purchase and raze two adjacent crack houses and to build additional classrooms. Student achievement scores also increased significantly (e.g., math scores went from the 14th to the 57th percentile; language arts from the 9th to the 39th percentile). On the other hand, the worst case to date was also a charter school within Los Angeles, Edutrain. This school had its charter revoked within a few months of opening for alleged financial mismanagement: a larger number of students were being reported than were actually in attendance, an expensive staff retreat was held in Carmel, and the principal was leasing a sports car with school funds (Lubman, 1994). The upside is that Edutrain is the only charter school to date (out of over 200 in operation) to get itself into this type of trouble, and the charter was revoked quickly.

Component #6: *There should be no limits on the number of charter schools that can be established within a given state.* Allowing just a handful of charter schools, when compared to the state's overall student population, communicates a lack of commitment to the reform. Individual charter organizers may think, ''Why bother?'' if indeed only a small number may be formed. Such limits are often the result of political compromises needed to enact the law. Although no state has yet reached the limit as established in law, such compromises weaken the law. (Note: As of July 1995, California had approved eighty-nine of 100 allowable charter schools, while Massachusetts has approved twenty-one of a total of twenty-five charter schools permitted by law.)

Component #7: *Charter schools must be permitted to employ noncertified teachers.* This component is critical because it challenges one of the educational system's most strongly held beliefs and brings additional expertise to the classroom. The completion of a set number of college of education-based courses and a student teaching practicum has long been the standard required to be considered ''fit'' to teach (in addition to a fingerprint check and passage of a basic skills test in a number of states). Teachers must often also acquire a set number of graduate-level courses to maintain their certification. Universities benefit from the steady stream of students (especially at the graduate level), while the teaching profession benefits by becoming a "closed shop."

The allowance of a certain percentage of noncertificated individuals within a charter school does not mean that anyone off the street should be placed into the classroom. Instead, it tests whether a focus on results, rather than inputs (e.g., certified teachers) is achievable in public education. When a school is placed on a contract, will it still choose to include only certified teachers or might it include some part-time specialists such as retired engineers or college professors? Stronger charter school laws allow this and other questions to be tested.

CURRENT STATUS OF CHARTER SCHOOL LAWS

Table 8.2 depicts how the seven components of a strong charter school law are distributed across the nineteen initial charter school states. One can see that only three of these states to date—Arizona, Delaware, and New Hampshire—have charter school laws that contain each of the essential provisions. Within these states, the charter school has full authority over its employees: who is hired and dismissed, what salaries will be, the number of contract days, as well as other employment provisions. These schools also have control over funds generated by their student count and may purchase services on the competitive market, not just from their local school district. They can be started and operated by individuals and entities other than traditional public school teachers (e.g., boys and girls clubs, social service providers). They can also hire individuals who do not have traditional teacher certificates, without having to participate in a special alternative program or seeking a waiver. Within six states—Massachusetts, Michigan, Texas, California, Minnesota, and Colorado—one or more of the seven key components is absent, although an alternate sponsor or appeals process is present and the resulting charter schools tend to be fiscally and legally autonomous entities. In the remaining ten states, most of the key components are missing. Laws in these states (with the exception of Louisiana, which is primarily only missing the non-local board sponsor component) do little to challenge the status quo or to create internal and external pressures for change. It is obvious that the manner in which the charter school concept has been operationalized in many states has resulted in a very

TABLE 8.2 *Initial charter school laws: analysis of "stronger" components.*[1]

	AZ ('94)	DE ('95)	NH ('95)	MA ('93)	MI ('94)	TX[2] ('95)	CA ('92)	MN ('91)	CO ('93)	LA ('95)	WI[3] ('93)	HI ('94)	WY ('95)	NM ('93)	RI ('95)	GA ('93)	KS ('94)	AR ('95)	AK ('95)
	⇦ -------- Stronger -------- ----- Weaker ----------- ⇨																		
1) Non-local board sponsor available or appeal process exists	x	x			x	x		x	x					x	x				
2) Any individual or group can attempt to organize a charter proposal	x	x		x	2	x	x	x	x	x	x		x				x		x
3) Automatic exemptions from most state laws/rules and local policies	x	x	x	x	x	x	x	x		x	3	x							
4) Fiscal autonomy—school has complete control over funds generated by their student count (including salaries)	x	x	x	x	x	4	x	x	5	x		x							

(continued)

TABLE 8.2 (*continued*).

	AZ ('94)	DE ('95)	NH ('95)	MA ('93)	MI ('94)	TX[2] ('95)	CA ('92)	MN ('91)	CO ('93)	LA ('95)	WI[3] ('93)	HI ('94)	WY ('95)	NM ('93)	RI ('95)	GA ('93)	KS ('94)	AR ('95)	AK ('95)
⇦ -------- Stronger --- Weaker -------- ⇧																			
5) legal autonomy (e.g., teachers are employees of school, not local district) or the charter (not the law) determines the level of legal autonomy	x	x	x	x	x	x	x	x	[5]	x									
6) No (or very high) limits on the number of charter schools that can be formed (compared to the total population)	x	x	x		x				x		x	x	x			x		x	

120

TABLE 8.2 *(continued)*.

	AZ ('94)	DE ('95)	NH ('95)	MA ('93)	MI ('94)	TX[2] ('95)	CA ('92)	MN ('91)	CO ('93)	LA ('95)	WI[3] ('93)	HI ('94)	WY ('95)	NM ('93)	RI ('95)	GA ('93)	KS ('94)	AR ('95)	AK ('95)
⇦ ------- Stronger														Weaker ------- ⇨					
7) Some percent noncertified individuals can teach at charter school (w/out having to seek a waiver or alt. certification)	x	6	x	x	7	x	x			x									
Total "Stronger" Components	7	7	7	6	6	6	6	5	5	5	3	3	3	2	1	1	1	1	1

[1] "Stronger" charter school law components are those that are most true to the charter school concept, tend to challenge the status quo aspects of the system, and theoretically may lead to broader student impacts and ripple effects. Component #1 (availability of non-local board sponsorship or appeal) is considered a vital component in order to get an adequate number of charter schools started.

[2] Based upon the "open enrollment" charter school portion of Texas's charter school bill. Eligible organizers are limited to public or private higher ed. institutions, a nonprofit, or a governmental entity.

[3] In Wisconsin, charter schools are automatically exempt from most state laws and rules, not local board policies. Also, recently enacted provisions strengthen the law for potential charter schools within the Milwaukee district only in that such schools can become legally and financially autonomous and have access to an appeal process involving the new state secretary of education.

[4] California's charter schools are allowed by law to be legally and fiscally autonomous, but this depends upon the provisions of a given school's charter.

[5] Legally, Colorado's charter schools are to remain a part of the local school and to receive at least 80% of their funds; in practice, however, many are operating quite autonomously.

[6] In Delaware, up to 35% noncertified teachers may be utilized if no qualified alternative certification program exists (and presently there is no such program in the state).

[7] In Michigan, the issue of automatic law exemptions is still unclear, and certification is required except in university-sponsored schools wherein higher education faculty can teach.

watered down ''cure'' at best. This is just one of many issues that will be examined in the next section.

OPPOSING FORCES

As profiled in the previous section, the reform elements embedded within the charter school concept are sound and appear promising—both as a means to better serve students and as a means of putting pressure on public education to reform—yet there are a number of forces that are working against the ultimate success of these schools. Some forces are due to the overlay of charter schools onto an existing education and school financing structure. Others are due to the vast resources and lobbying efforts of special interest groups that are trying to water down or derail any true reform efforts. Still others involve the lack of an entrepreneurial spirit among the vast majority of educators. We will briefly examine these and other issues to reveal just how strong these collective forces are.

The overall number of states with strong charter school laws is too small to make a significant difference. As noted previously, the number of charter school states with ''stronger'' laws on the books is still quite small. Although several of these ''stronger'' states are some of the most populous, Texas currently only allows twenty fully autonomous charter schools to be created, while California allows 100—a small fraction of the total number of public schools in each state. Efforts to increase these numbers are underway, but the total number of allowable charters will probably remain low due to political pressures. Until a significant number of states enact stronger charter school laws, too small a fraction of the educational arena will be touched by these schools, much less impacted.

There is a lack of organized, well-financed support for the charter school movement. Since the charter school concept represents a blend of ideas and often has appeal across party lines, it has no clearly defined constituency to support the growth of the movement. Many groups that openly advocate for private school vouchers view charter schools as ''second best.'' The creation of charter schools introduces some of the competition they want, but not as much as if private and religious schools were to become part of the reform. Therefore, any funds that such groups have available for advocacy continue to be focused on the push for vouchers, not charter schools.

On the other side, well-financed teachers' unions and school board associations only support charter schools to the extent that they are a means to ward off private school vouchers. These groups are clearly not spending any funds to support the growth of the charter concept—especially stronger laws—and, indeed, continue to spend significant amounts to defeat or weaken pending legislation. For example, the director of City Academy Charter School in Minnesota—who happens to remain a member of the National Education Association (NEA)—noted that she was recently informed that NEA had spent over $12 million to defeat charter school legislation (M. Cutter, personnel communication, July 13, 1995). Her membership dues were being used to ultimately undermine the success of her charter school! Further, it was noted that the American Federation of Teachers (AFT) had spent over $3 million to defeat charter schools. It is impossible to verify whether these figures are high or low, but these authors have seen firsthand in several states—Arizona, Louisiana, Texas, and Florida—efforts by the NEA and AFT state affiliates, as well as the school boards association, to defeat the charter school movement.

In contrast, funding to promote the concept of charter schools has been limited. Some corporate and foundation funding has been made, although most has been earmarked to help existing charter schools (a key exception to this is a recent Hudson Institute project funded by the Pew Charitable Trusts to analyze charter school startup and policy issues). Also, Congress appropriated $6 million in 1994 to provide startup funds and to evaluate individual charter schools. Technical assistance and startup funds are indeed an important means to support the charter school concept since successful schools are perhaps the best selling point; however, they do little to derail a well-financed lobbying campaign against the concept. Overall, there are some efforts by various groups to educate policymakers, educators, and the public in the hopes of building a constituency of support for the concept, but these are small in scale when compared to the resources of the opposition.

Those groups opposed to the charter school concept are becoming more sophisticated in their opposition. As new states enter the debate on charter schools, it is becoming clear that those opposed to the concept are changing tactics. As noted by Kolderie (1995), the new strategy is to support or promote ''weak'' charter legislation, rather than simply trying to kill the bill completely. A weak charter school bill has the benefits of holding voucher proponents at bay (at least for a bit), yet initial activities reveal that little chartering activity occurs in those states with weak laws. Indeed, of the eight states that most recently passed charter school laws (during 1995), five fell into the weaker side of the spectrum (see Table 8.2). One would think that legislators who strongly believe in the concept would have learned from the initial states—a weak charter school law is perhaps worse than no law at all. However, given the lack of a well-financed effort to disseminate this information, those opposed to charter schools have the upper hand.

One example reveals the growing sophistication of those who oppose charter schools. Louisiana's initial charter school bill stated that any existing district's collective bargaining provisions would *not* apply to those within the charter school, unless specifically called for in the charter. An amendment was offered proposing that such provisions *would* apply to charter schools unless the charter specifically abolished them. This amendment appeared harmless to many legislators (and it passed), but its impact is significant. Charter school organizers in this state must now start with existing bargaining provisions as a given and work to remove specific items of concern.

The opposition is also fighting to keep charter schools under the control of local school boards. One can see why school board associations would want this provision, but why the teachers' unions? One reason is that teachers unions have great influence over their local school boards and only limited power in reference to state boards and universities. However, even in those cases where their battle was lost at the legislative level, pressure continues to be applied elsewhere. For example, a school superintendent in Michigan recently sent a letter to Central Michigan University (CMU) stating that the district would no longer accept student teachers from that university nor recommend that its graduates attend CMU (Allen, 1995). The Michigan Education Association offered similar threats but later backed down once they were made public. What had CMU done to provoke such threats? They had chartered over thirty schools in their state and are actively working with more.

Charter schools are being forced to operate within state school financing structures that were designed to fund districts, not schools. A key tenet of a charter school is that those involved in the school will have control over all funds generated by its student count. In reality, however, no charter school to date has gained access to this entire sum of money. At most, they receive the "operations" funds provided per student as part of a state financing formula. They do not have access to funding for large capital items (such as facilities), or special program funds that are often distributed on a district basis, rather than on a per pupil basis (e.g., substance abuse funds, federal Title I funds). In addition, some laws specify that the charter school has to negotiate with the district to determine how much of the per pupil operations funding they will receive. Districts are often not supportive since they see charter schools as taking *their* students and *their* funding. Overall, the current financing structure in which charter schools are being asked to operate acts as a major force against their success.

Of key concern is the lack of funding for facilities. The acquisition and maintenance of school buildings generally comes from the sale of bonds by the district. Repayment of these bonds, in turn, is supported through a district taxing mechanism. Since charter schools do not have definite boundaries and often draw their student population from across district lines, they have not been given taxing authority to generate revenues for buildings. Thus, charter schools begin their struggle for survival with significantly less funding per student than regular public schools. Yet they must still find a facility in which to operate their school, often taking out leases on retail space, old church buildings, community recreational centers, and the like. In some cases, districts have been supportive and offered them school buildings, although these buildings were often no longer deemed appropriate for regular district use. Some charter schools have been fortunate to find a local university or business that is willing to loan them a good facility at no (or low) cost. Others must find buildings and spend large amounts of "operations" funds to upgrade facilities to meet health and safety codes. Still others with approved charter contracts have failed to open their doors because an adequate facility could not be found.

Only a small fraction of the current education profession has the interest and motivation to undertake the implementation of a charter school. The current education profession does not attract large percentages of individuals who have an entrepreneurial spirit. Given the past nature of the industry, those who are often most successful are those who do not rock the boat or question the current governance structure. Therefore, there are few existing teachers and school-level administrators who have the inclination or wherewithal to operate a successful charter school (perhaps no more than 5 – 10 percent). This factor, compounded by pending lawsuits in several states, the finicky nature of politicians who could easily undo a charter law at anytime, and the continued opposition by their professional associations, has discouraged many educators with an interest in charter schools from becoming involved.

For those who have chosen to take on the challenge of a charter school, many are becoming worn out. These individuals are attempting to take on both the instructional and management aspects of schooling, with little professional assistance available to them. Existing training and university programs were not developed to meet their specific needs. Other entities such as the Internal Revenue Service, state retirement systems, regional purchasing cooperatives, state departments of education, and even the NEA did not initially know how to classify these new public entities. Nearly every charter school operator has stories that focus on being told that something cannot be done. Even in states wherein nearly all state laws and rules have been removed, the existing structures that had created those laws and rules have not been removed. Barriers are put up every step along the way. Having to be held to a level of student outcome accountability unheard of within the public school sector, as well as breaking down numerous barriers, may prove too much for the best of them.

There is a question of whether unbiased research of charter schools can and will be conducted by those traditionally involved in K – 12 education research. Although most researchers claim objectivity in their work, human nature limits the extent to which individuals can distance themselves from a chosen topic. A researcher approaches a study with a set of assumptions and theories that guide the study and determine what is to be tested. These hypotheses are often derived from traditional educational practice. Since the charter school concept so strongly challenges current practice, researchers may have difficulty drawing conclusions based solely on the data collected from the study, and not on biases that they may unconsciously (or consciously) bring with them. Hidden agendas such as publicity may also be at work.

A specific example will highlight these points. A recent study by Southwest Regional Laboratory (SWRL), ''Parent Involvement Contracts in California's Charter Schools: Strategy for Educational Improvement or Method of Exclusion?'' (Becker et al., 1995), is being questioned by many involved with these schools. This report examines issues surrounding the parent contracts often used by charter schools, and many of its findings were quite favorable toward charter schools, including:

(1) ''On all nine measures — from parent attendance at school functions, special programs, and classes, to helping in the classroom or elsewhere in the building, to doing major committee work, to fundraising and other leadership roles — a higher proportion of parents in the charter schools were reported to be participants than parents in the comparison schools'' (p. 6).

(2) ''Teacher-specific practices . . . indicate a consistence and substantial difference between efforts by teachers in charter and comparison schools to involve parents at home. On every measure taken, charter school teachers are reported to be more active'' (p. 9).

However, the report's title and abstract send the message that some charter schools may be excluding ''less desirable students'' by virtue of their parent contracts. This conclusion was despite another finding that ''charter schools with parent contracts had roughly the same level of parent involvement on these measures as did charter schools without such contracts'' (p. 7). When questioned about the negative focus of the title and abstract, the primary author responded: ''The editorial staff of SWRL, in writing the abstract, chose to emphasize only the more critical aspects highlighted in the discussion section, which does not fairly represent the balance of analyses contained in the paper'' (H. Becker, personal communication, July 7, 1995). Given that the report's title and abstract were picked up by the press across the state, one has to wonder about the motives of those who chose to emphasize this component.

This example raises concerns about all future research on charter schools, not just studies that spotlight negative conclusions. For example, another recent study (involving charter schools in Colorado) drew overall positive conclusions, but questions of potential bias also need to be raised. The researcher examined the first year of implementation for Colorado's charter schools and concluded that the concept was well received, as evidenced by long waiting lists at many of the schools, the attraction of some students back from the private schools, and the overall excitement of those involved in the charters (Fitzgerald, 1995). However, the report was financed by the Colorado Children's Campaign, one of the state's leading proponents of charter schools. Would the report have been disseminated widely if the results had been negative?

A federally funded evaluation of charter schools (which began during fall 1995) also illustrates this concern. Many of the leading school reform researchers competed for the opportunity to conduct this evaluation research; however, nearly every individual and group that submitted a proposal could be pegged into a "sort-of charter school supporter" or a "sort-of-not charter school supporter" based upon their past research foci. The charter school concept questions so much of our traditional beliefs regarding public education and reform that truly unbiased research simply may not be possible. This is unfortunate for the many teachers, parents, and policymakers who want to know whether these schools will make a difference. Given the ongoing demand by charter school critics for "proof," it represents one more force that undermines the potential success of charter schools.

CAN THE ODDS BE BEATEN?

We have painted a rather bleak picture for the long-term future of charter schools. Whether this prediction will become fact is too early to tell, but an analysis of the forces operating against charter schools provides insight into the problem with many other reforms. Reforms must fit within the current power structure of education: local school boards, state boards of education, state departments, legislators, the federal government, and unions. The current power structure seeks to mold legislation to meet its needs, not necessarily the needs of students, and it is difficult to break down this ingrained system of power.

In theory, charter schools attempt to break down the ingrained status quo elements of the system, and in reality, a great deal has already been accomplished. Over 420 charter schools are already in operation. Many students who had not been successful in the traditional public school setting are now excelling. Unique community and business partnerships are being formed, with many traditional "outsiders" becoming intimately involved in the public educational arena. Most importantly, ripple effects across the broader system are becoming visible as districts respond to pressures created by charter schools. Indeed, even the National Education Association has recently launched a national support project for those attempting to implement charter schools. However, the odds are stacked against the ultimate success of charter schools. Unless well-coordinated efforts are undertaken to battle the many opposing forces, we predict that the charter school concept will simply not be strong enough medicine to become a broad-based reform initiative.

REFERENCES

Allen, J. (1995, June). *Monthly newsletter,* Washington, D.C.: The Center for Education Reform.

Becker, H. J., Nakagawa, K. and Corwin, R. (1995, April). *Parental involvement contracts in California's charter schools: Strategy for educational improvement of method of exclusion?* Los Alamitos, CA: Southwest Regional Laboratory.

Bierlein, L. and Mulholland, L. (1994, September). The promise of charter schools. *Educational Leadership,* pp. 34–40.

Bell, T. (1995). The charter-school plus. *Education Week,* March 15, p. 40.

Fitzgerald, J. (1995, March). *Charter schools in Colorado.* Denver, CO: Colorado Children's Campaign.

Fuhrman, S. H. and Elmore, R. F. (1995, March). *Ruling out rules: The evolution of deregulation in state education policy.* New Brunswick, NJ: Rutgers, The State University of New Jersey, Consortium for Policy Research in Education.

Kolderie, T. (1995). *The charter idea in the 1995 legislative sessions.* St. Paul, MN: Center for Policy Studies.

Lubman, S. (1994, December 7). Charter is revoked for local school of Los Angeles. *The Wall Street Journal,* p. A4.

Mulholland, L. and Bierlein, L. (1995, April). *Understanding charter schools* (Fastback #383). Bloomington, IN: Phi Delta Kappa Educational Foundation.

Porterfield, B. (1994, February 20). Texas doing homework on charter school concept. *The Austin American-Statesman,* p. A1.

Raywid, M. A. (1995, March). The struggles and joys of trailblazing: A tale of two charter schools. *Phi Delta Kappan* 76(7):555–560

Quinn, R. (1993, August). Charter schools: Now what? *Colorado Association of School Boards (CASB) Agenda,* p. 2.

CHAPTER 9

School Finance Litigation: The Merry-Go-Round Reform

Indeed, the repeat litigation in such states as New Jersey and Connecticut, as those school systems fail to meet constitutional standards year after year, indicates how difficult it is to put judicial mandates into practice.

—Alexandra Natapoff (1994)

By the late 1960s, any observant person could see that there were vast disparities in the financial resources available to school districts in many of the states. These disparities, it was apparent, were a direct result of the way schools were funded during that time. In almost every state, school districts depended on local property taxes for the lion's share of their annual revenues. In districts that had relatively large amounts of valuable property on their tax roles, schools could be funded at a high level. But in those districts that were property-poor, schools had a smaller tax base to rely on; consequently, fewer revenues were available for public education.

In some instances, the disparity in resources between school districts was shocking. In California, for example, the state's wealthiest high school district had twenty-nine times as much taxable property per student as did the state's poorest school district. Obviously, disparities of this magnitude lead to significant differences in educational programs from district to district.

During this period, a handful of scholars began developing legal theories to challenge school funding inequities in court. Arthur Wise was

131

the first to take up this task. In *Rich Schools, Poor Schools* (1968), Wise developed an argument that the funding inequities that arose from a reliance on property taxes was unconstitutional. Wise drew upon precedents from three areas in which the United States Supreme Court had articulated constitutional standards to initiate reforms: desegregation, reapportionment, and the rights of persons accused of crimes. Building upon these legal precedents, Wise formulated this simple principle: "A child's educational opportunity should be independent of his parents' circumstances and where he happens to live within a state" (p. xiii).

Wise's work was followed closely by the seminal work of law Professor John E. Coons and two of his students, William Clune and Stephen Sugarman. In 1969, Coons, Clune, and Sugarman published a much cited law review article that articulated a constitutional standard against which to test state educational finance structures. They developed the principle of fiscal neutrality, which held that "the quality of public education may not be a function of wealth other than the wealth of the state as a whole" (p. 311). This legal theory was soon to be tested in their home state of California.

A QUARTER CENTURY OF LITIGATION

Little did John Serrano know that his discussion with his son's principal in 1967 would help to launch an educational reform effort that would leave no state untouched by its pursuit for change. He started a reform that has many of the characteristics of a merry-go-round carousel in which there is a lot of movement: riders can change horses and new riders can join the carousel. But the riders never arrive at a final destination; they can just go around again and again.

Mr. Serrano's son attended public school in Los Angeles. When Mr. Serrano complained about the quality of available school services, the principal told him that the school district could not afford more and that if he wanted more for his son he would have to move to a wealthier school district. Unfortunately, Mr. Serrano could not move. Instead, he and several others brought suit in California state court against several state officials. The real target of the suit was not the individual officials but, rather, the whole state system of public education funding. The resulting court case, *Serrano v. Priest* (1971), not only changed the way California funds public education, but it also ushered in an era of reform—school finance reform.

The California Supreme Court in *Serrano* found that the state's system for financing schools depended on the property tax base of each school district. Consequently, vast differences in property wealth between school districts created substantial differences in revenues available for expenditures on resources and programs for students. Those students who were fortunate enough to have parents who live in an area with high property values had more educational opportunities, better facilities, more supplies and equipment, and generally more expansive course offerings than students who lived in districts with low property wealth.[1]

Since education is a state responsibility, it was reasoned that the state must treat its citizens, including minors, equally when discharging its legal responsibilities. According to the court, tying school funding to property wealth through the use of property taxes, interjects the idiosyncrasy of local circumstances into a state responsibility of providing education to its citizens. For example, as Slavin (1994) noted, ''A factory closing can bankrupt a small school district. What sense does it make for children's education to suffer based on local accidents or geography or economics?'' (p. 98). Since children in California had unequal educational opportunities because of their personal geography—where they lived—and the state through its constitution has the responsibility for educating its citizens, the court, therefore, reasoned that California's scheme for financing public education by relying on property taxes violated state and federal equal protection guarantees. Echoing Arthur Wise in his work *Rich Schools, Poor Schools* (1968), the court stated that the gross funding disparities between school districts unconstitutionally made education ''a function of [the child's] parents and neighbors'' (p. 589). The state's heavy reliance on property taxes to fund schools was found to be unconstitutional. The California Supreme Court ordered the state to reduce the disparity between school districts' per pupil expenditures. The impetus behind the decision was to assure more equity in per pupil expenditures.

However, in 1973, in *San Antonio Independent School District v. Rodriguez,* the United States Supreme Court ruled that education was not a fundamental right under the United States Constitution, thus precluding plaintiffs from attacking inequitable school funding systems in the federal courts. In *Rodriguez,* the Supreme Court made it clear that it was not placing its "judicial imprimatur" on the practice of using property taxes to fund schools. Indeed, Justice Stewart, in a concurring opinion, described the Texas finance system as "chaotic and unjust." The Court noted that the "need is apparent for reform in tax systems which may well have relied too long and too heavily on the local property tax" (pp. 58–59). Rather, the Court determined that the effort to bring greater uniformity of opportunity in school finance should come from the state, not the federal level of government.

After the *Rodriguez* decision, legal challenges against state education funding were presented in the state courts. Only a few days after the Supreme Court issued its decision in *Rodriguez,* the New Jersey Supreme Court overturned New Jersey's system of school finance, relying solely on the educational clause in the state constitution (*Robinson v. Cahill,* 1973). In the years to come, other state supreme courts decided school finance cases. To this day, lawsuits over school funding are still being battled in state courts.

MORE WAVES OF REFORM–FROM EQUITY TO ADEQUACY

McCarthy (1994) notes that most major school finance reform efforts have been prodded by or accompanied by litigation in which the state had been sued. Since *Rodriguez,* reformers have turned to state courts and focused on state constitutional guarantees to invalidate funding schemes that resulted in great disparities in expenditures between school districts. A wave of school finance cases flowed across the nation from California to New Jersey from 1971 to the time of the release of *A Nation at Risk* (National Commission on Excellence in Education, 1983). These cases, in nineteen states, focused primarily on the disparities in educational expenditures across school districts in a state and on the relationship between the revenue and the property wealth of the school districts. In other words, plaintiffs argued that state school funding schemes led to unconstitutional inequities in the way school districts were financed.

Of the nineteen cases, ten state courts declared that the school finance formulas were constitutional, whereas nine courts declared their state's formula unconstitutional. In five of these states, in the first wave of school finance reform, each rode the litigation carousel twice – California 1971, 1976; Pennsylvania 1979, 1987; West Virginia 1979, 1988; Ohio 1979, 1994; and New York 1982, 1987. More states were to join the carousel ride with the second wave of finance reform, most notably Texas, with four trips to court.

The equity argument of the first wave of school finance reform was a formidable argument. Equity and equality are treasured concepts in the American psyche. An equity argument tends to take and hold the moral high ground in policy debates. Congressman Hawkins (1991) noted the ideological benefits of this argument when he wrote, ''The concept of equality is deeply embedded in our national ethos. We Americans love to be seen as good sports who guarantee a fair chance for all'' (p. 565). The equity argument in school finance litigation touched a resonant chord much like the equality argument in *Brown v. Board of Education* did for desegregation.

While the courts in nineteen states argued over disparities in educational funding during the decade between *Serrano* and *A Nation at Risk* (National Commission on Excellence in Education, 1983) a major change in funding took place in America's public schools. First, funding from all sources – federal, state, and local governments – increased an average of 12 percent (adjusted for inflation). Second, by the end of the 1970s, the states, for the first time in history, had become the major providers of revenue for education, providing nearly 50 percent of the revenue (Verstegen, 1994). This shift in funding is the logical outcome of funding equity litigation. The only way that revenue disparities between school districts in a state can be eliminated is for the state to provide the bulk of funding so that a more equitable distribution can be assured. Since *Rodriguez* stated that education was not a federal fundamental right, it became clear that only the states, through their redistribution ability, could bring about a leveling or narrowing of the funding gap. This increased presence of state funding not only occurred in those states where the funding litigation was successful, but it also happened in states where funding litigation was threatened. Whether it was intended or not, the movement of control from the local level to the state level was an outcome of early school finance litigation that sought funding equity between school districts.

School finance litigation was quiet, almost dormant during the mid 1980s. Possibly the nation was caught up in other reform efforts spurred by the *A Nation at Risk* report. Whatever the reason, it was not until around 1989 that a second wave of school finance litigation burst upon the national scene. Starting in the second wave, litigants and courts broadened their focus to include, not only concerns about funding equity, but concerns about the overall adequacy of education funding as well. The rationale behind this new emphasis was that equal, but inadequate, funding could not reform education. Where equity focused on inputs—per pupil expenditures—adequacy focused on educational outcomes.

In essence, the adequacy argument shifted the focus beyond dollar disparities to what the dollar buys—teachers, administrators, curriculum, facilities, and programs. Sufficiency of resources to provide quality educational programs, services, and opportunities to learn became the major considerations in this new wave of reform litigation (Verstegen, 1994). Instead of just comparing school districts' per pupil expenditures, the courts were considering whether the state was providing the level of education that was necessary for productive citizenship and competition in the labor market. Adequacy redefined the level of education a state must provide and used new measurement tools and criteria for compliance.

For example, adequacy arguments in the various states pointed out the devastating, appalling, and totally unacceptable conditions that existed in many of the schools that were parties to these lawsuits. Pictures of unsanitary conditions, broken windows, cracked tiles, and peeling paint were entered into evidence at trials throughout the nation. In Alabama, it was noted that teachers routinely use trash cans as buckets to catch rainwater that poured through holes in the ceiling of their classrooms. In Tennessee, a school library reportedly consisted of a single bookcase (Natapoff, 1994). Such examples were grist for the adequacy argument mill and provided an avenue of attack on state finance systems that was not available under an equity argument.

In addition to finance reform, adequacy prompted systemic change. For example, in the landmark case, *Rose v. The Council for Better Education, Inc.* (1989), the Kentucky Supreme Court found the entire state system of education to be unconstitutional and consequently dismantled it, leaving the legislature the task of creating it anew. In Tennessee, the state supreme court held that school finance was inadequate, unequal, and unconstitutional. This prompted the passage of Tennessee's Educational Improvement Act. Likewise, on June 18, 1993, Governor Weld signed a ninety-seven-page bill entitled the Massachusetts Educational Reform Act of 1993. The governor's signature came only a few days after the Massachusetts Supreme Judicial Court, in *McDuffy v. Secretary of the Executive Office of Education* (1993), declared the system of education finance to be unconstitutional. All three of these school finance cases prompted large-scale reform in their respective states.

Probably the best example of the breadth of the adequacy argument is Kentucky's *Rose* (1989) case, which found that the Kentucky system failed to meet its constitutional obligation to educate all its children. In articulating the standard of education that the state must strive to achieve, the Kentucky Supreme Court adopted seven attributes of an educated child. An educated child, the court said, must have these capabilities: (1) sufficient oral and written communication skills to enable the student to function in a complex and rapidly changing civilization; (2) sufficient knowledge of economic, social, and political systems to enable the student to make informed decisions; (3) sufficient understanding of governmental processes to enable the student to understand the issues that affect his or her community, state, and nation; (4) sufficient self-knowledge and knowledge of his or her mental and physical wellness; (5) sufficient grounding in the arts to enable each student to appreciate his or her cultural and historical heritage; (6) sufficient training or preparation for advances in either academic or vocational fields so as to enable each child to choose and pursue life work intelligently; and (7) sufficient level of academic or vocational skills to enable public school students to compete favorably with their counterparts in surrounding states, in academics, or in the job market. The applicability of these attributes and the strength of the underlying adequacy argument was attested to when the Massachusetts Supreme Judicial Court adopted these attributes in *McDuffy*.

This wave of reform, led by the adequacy argument, rolled over the nation. But the carousel-like quality of school finance reform found in the first wave also surfaced in the second wave. New Jersey found itself once again litigating school finance reform much as it did in the first

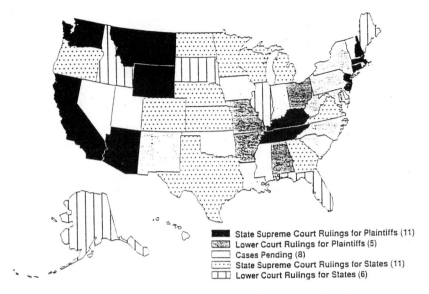

Figure 9.1 *Map of status of school finance lawsuits. (*Source: Education Week, *February 15, 1995, p. 11.)*

wave. In Texas, school finance litigants went to the Texas Supreme Court four times between 1989 and 1995, as the state legislature made successive attempts to pass a school funding formula that would pass constitutional muster (Sparkman & Hartmeister, 1995). Lawyers in West Virginia are reopening a school finance case, which in the 1980s had been hailed as a major step toward ending funding disparities in the state. For over twenty years, many states have wrestled with school finance reform, without bringing the issue to closure (Figure 9.1). In many cases, school funding litigation has brought more dollars to underfunded school districts and reduced the inequity between poor and wealthy schools. But these waves of litigation have not improved the overall quality of education in the nation's most poorly performing schools.

QUALITY EDUCATION: DOES MONEY MATTER?

As Underwood observes: "All plaintiffs in school finance litigation rely on the common assumption that the level of funding of a school district has a direct effect on the quality of the program provided and the education children receive'' (1989, pp. 414–415). But is this assumption valid? If just increasing the level of funding cures the ills that beset public education, why are some children still receiving an inadequate education, even after more money was invested in the schools? The question strikes at the heart of the reform—if money does not matter, what are we arguing about in court?

At the same time courts were engaging in a constitutional analysis of state systems of school finance, some scholars were challenging the notion that money matters in producing quality education. In *Equality of Educational Opportunity,* commonly known as the ''Coleman Report,'' Coleman and his colleagues (1966), after surveying and testing 600,000 students in over 3,000 schools across the nation, concluded that the socioeconomic background of the student influenced achievement more than schools. Pursuing this line of reasoning and research, Hanushek's (1989) synthesis of over thirty-eight articles and books on the education production function (school inputs and student outputs) found no direct relationship between money and the quality of a child's education. While studying the relationship between expenditures and student performance, he noted that real school expenditures more than doubled during a twenty-year period when SAT scores declined. Looking at such inputs as teacher-student ratios, teacher education, teacher experience, administration, and facilities, Hanushek concluded that ''there is no strong or systematic relationship between school expenditures and student performance'' (p. 47). Similarly, Silber, the president of Boston University, noted that per pupil expenditures in the Boston Public Schools were more than twice the amount spent by the Springfield, Massachusetts schools, a system of roughly the same quality and beset by the same kinds of problems. Yet both districts had similar mediocre standardized test scores. This proves, Silber (1990) dryly observed, ''that you can have bad schools for far less money'' (p. 35).

However, other scholars have argued persuasively that money can improve schooling. For example, Ferguson (1991) published the results of research that supports the commonsense judgment that increased education funding, when targeted and managed wisely, can improve the quality of education for students. Based on a massive study of more than

900 Texas school districts with a combined enrollment of 2.4 million students, Ferguson reached two major conclusions. First, lower pupil/teacher ratios are correlated to better student test scores, controlling for a number of family and community background factors. Second, teachers' salaries, when compared to the salaries of nearby districts, are an important factor when teachers make a decision about where to teach. In other words, a school district must pay a competitive salary if it wishes to attract the best teachers.

In *Who Will Teach? Policies That Matter,* Murnane et al. (1991) identified another way in which money can make a difference in the quality of schooling. Murnane's research describes how salary increases, when used to retain teachers in the early years of teaching, affect student learning patterns. Although his research demonstrated that years of experience may enhance student performance, there is a certain time threshold where seniority has no further impact.

Richard Rothstein (1993), in an insightful article that appeared in *The American Prospect,* entered the "Does Money Matter?" debate from a different perspective. Responding to critics who argue that increased spending has not improved educational outcomes, Rothstein said, in essence, that little new money has been invested in regular education over the past twenty-five years.

"Spending hasn't failed," Rothstein wrote. "It hasn't been tried" (1993, p. 85). When money spent on special new programs is subtracted from the nation's total investment in education, he argued, it becomes clear that little of the growth in public education spending has gone to the regular classroom.

Rothstein calculated that nearly 30 percent of new education money has gone to special education programs for children with disabilities. About 12 percent of all school children are now enrolled in various special education programs, and the per pupil cost of these programs is roughly double the cost of regular education for a nondisabled child. It is dishonest, Rothstein argued, to suggest that special education funds should produce academic gains for nondisabled students and, when they do not, to claim proof that money spent on public schools is wasted.

In addition to reviewing the new costs associated with special education, Rothstein also noted that nearly 10 percent of the increased cost of public education is attributable to the school lunch and breakfast programs. Salary increases for teachers account for some of the increased costs—about 8 percent—according to Rothstein's calculations. Also, more students are bused than was the case twenty-five years ago, and the cost of additional busing accounts for another 5 percent of the increased costs. Finally, according to Rothstein, American schools on the whole have cut the school drop-out rate, which means schools are incurring some additional costs in educating students who would have been dropouts in the 1960s.

Rothstein's arguments are in harmony with a report issued by researchers at the Sandia National Laboratories in 1992 and published in the *Journal of Educational Research* in 1993 (Carson et al., 1993). The Sandia researchers concluded that American public education had succeeded in gradually lowering drop-out rates over a twenty-year period and, in general, had improved standardized test scores. Moreover, the researchers agreed with Rothstein that a substantial portion of the increased expenditures for education have been devoted to special education, not the regular education classroom.

In short, the scholarly retort to the argument that money does not matter when it comes to improving educational outcomes has made two solid points. First, increased expenditures, targeted wisely, have in fact had a good effect in many school environments. Second, much of the increased expenditures have gone to meet new school commitments such as special education, transportation, and the like—not to improving regular education.

Professor Murnane (1991), in an article about the impact of money on school performance, has also made a useful contribution to the "Does Money Matter?" debate. Money alone, Murnane pointed out, will not lead to higher student achievement if poorly performing school districts continue to engage in harmful practices—haphazard teacher recruiting, for example. "It would be a mistake," he argued, "for school finance reform strategies of the 1990s simply to aim at increasing expenditures in low spending districts" (p. 462). Increased funding can help improve schooling in some districts, but it will not help others "unless strategies are devised to change the way people interact" (Murnane, 1991, p. 462).

SCHOOL FINANCE REFORM AND ITS IMPACT

Today, 25 years after the *Serrano* decision declared the California school finance system to be unconstitutional, nearly every state in the nation has been involved in school finance reform litigation. This reform effort is a clear example of law-based mechanisms (litigation and legislation) being used as the vehicles to bring about reform. The amount of money spent on this litigation must be staggering. But what return on all of the expenditures of money, time, and energy have the nation's students received? The results are modest at best. Many states have climbed aboard the carousel of litigation and resulting legislation and gotten off only to climb aboard once again for another ride that probably will not take them anywhere new. The first wave of reform focused on inequality between rich and poor school districts. The second wave, formed when the first was found to be ineffectual, then aimed at making schools adequate. In the midst of these waves of reform, research studies questioned whether new moneys are the answer to the old question of how we achieve quality in our schools given the broad inclusive mission that society has assigned to it.

Without question, school finance litigation has helped shape education policy in important ways. First, because of *Serrano* and its progeny, it is now generally accepted that school funding is primarily a state, not a local, responsibility. Even in states where courts have rejected *Serrano*-type lawsuits, almost no one would contend that the funding of public education is entirely a local responsibility. Arthur Wise's once controversial proposition—that a child's educational opportunities should be independent of where he or she happens to live in a state—now finds wide acceptance.

Second, the need to reduce the disparities between school district per pupil expenditures necessitated a gathering of power at the state level. The states, with the exception of New Hampshire, provide a larger share of total school revenues than was the case twenty-five years ago. In 1970, the year before *Serrano* was decided, only about 40 percent of the total revenues were generated at the state level (Odden, 1992, p. 50). By the 1987–1988 school year, the figure was almost 50 percent (National Center for Education Statistics, 1994, p. 152).

Third, school finance litigation has contributed to the dramatic growth in overall public education funding over the past twenty-five years. In nominal dollars, school revenues have roughly doubled every ten years since 1960 (Odden, 1992, p. 10). Even adjusting for inflation, the growth has been substantial — a 30 percent increase between 1980 and 1990. Some of this growth would have taken place whether or not the school finance litigation had taken place. Nevertheless, school finance lawsuits exerted considerable pressure on legislatures to find more money for poor school districts, and this was true whether or not plaintiffs ultimately won their cases in the courts. In New Hampshire, the threat of a funding lawsuit, many believe, resulted in the state devising a new funding scheme called the Augenblick Formula.

Most observers would view these developments as positive. However, it is now clear that school finance lawsuits have not affected some of the core afflictions of public education in this country. Why is this the case?

First of all, some of the nation's most troubled school districts are not underfunded, and providing more money to them would probably not improve conditions by any measurable extent. New Jersey, for example, where the state's highest court first declared the New Jersey system of school funding to be unconstitutional in 1973, has some of the most seriously underperforming school districts in the country. The New Jersey Department of Education has found it necessary to take three of them over — Newark, Jersey City, and Patterson (McLarin, 1994).

The problems in some of these New Jersey districts include mismanagement or corruption — not lack of money. On the contrary, New Jersey funds its schools at a higher level than almost any other state — about $10,000 per pupil in some school districts. Indeed, the New Jersey Supreme Court acknowledged that money alone would not solve the problems of the state's failing schools, particularly in the inner cities. "The dilemma," the court wrote, "is that while we spend so much, there is absolutely no question that we are failing to provide the students in the poorer urban districts with the kind of an education that anyone would call thorough and efficient" (*Abbott v. Burke,* 1990, p. 412). Funding has increased in some situations, but quality education still eludes many school districts.

Second, although scholars can quarrel with some of the details of Hanushek's arguments about school funding, Hanushek (1989) is certainly right to point out that there is no certain correlation between increased expenditures and student outcomes. In Baton Rouge, Louisiana, for example, a system of about 60,000 students, annual expenditures increased from less than $40 million in 1967 to about a quarter of a billion dollars in 1991. In spite of this growth, which is fairly typical of urban school districts during this period, student on-time completion rates dropped from 73 percent in 1967 to 62 percent twenty-five years later. This is not to say that the Baton Rouge schools wasted the additional moneys it received. The district's at-risk student population grew substantially over the years, as did its special education population. It may well be that the district made wise financial decisions and that its on-time completion rate dropped in spite of its best efforts. But the Baton Rouge experience certainly illustrates the proposition that money alone will not improve public education in the United States.

Finally, it is becoming increasingly obvious that the main barrier to improved student outcomes in the nation's schools is not school spending, but the socioeconomic status of the child's family. For example, Cooley recently concluded, after a study of Pennsylvania school districts, that three indicators account for more than 60 percent of the variation in average student performance among districts: the percentages of children living in poverty, the percentage of adults who are not high school graduates, and the percentage of children living in single-parent homes (Sadowski, 1995). It seems unlikely that increased school funding will have more than a marginal impact on these factors.

Law-based mechanisms tried, but were not able, to meet all of the hopes of the reform effort. They served as a searchlight by focusing on the problems of unequal educational opportunities based on property wealth, inadequate facilities, and unacceptable student outcomes. Nevertheless, more money—or even more equitably distributed money—will not by itself improve the nation's schools. To their credit, some courts acknowledged, at least implicitly, that just throwing money at schools will not necessarily improve them. This is why, after addressing the inequities in school funding among school districts, many courts went on to articulate a standard of quality that students have a right to expect from their educational experience, quite apart from monetary considerations. Unfortunately, it is exactly this area—assuring educational quality—where the courts are least effective. It is one thing for the Kentucky Supreme Court to define the seven attributes of an educated child; it is quite another for the court to mandate that children be taught in such a way that they gain these attributes.

This is not to say that the era of school finance reform litigation has outlived its usefulness. Twenty-five years after the *Serrano* decision, litigation is ongoing in many states, including Louisiana, where some schools operate under appalling conditions, due in part to a lack of money. ''There is little doubt that increased funding alone does not guarantee improved student performance. There is also no question that money spent wisely can make a difference in the quality of education received by children in rich and poor schools'' (Conn, 1994, p. 23). But the limits of litigation as an educational reform strategy are now apparent. In some settings, educators need to shift away from a focus on more money, or even more equitably distributed money, and turn their attention to the hard work of determining how the presently available money can best be used to nurture and inspire children.

REFERENCES

Abbott v. Burke, 575 A.2d 359 (N.J. 1990).

Board of Education v. Walter, 390 N.E.2d 813 (1979).

Carson, C. C., Huelskamp, R. M., and Woodall, T. D. 1993. Perspectives on education in America. *Journal of Educational Research* 86:259–310.

Coleman, J. 1966. *Equality of educational opportunity.* Washington, D.C.: U.S. Government Printing Office.

Conn, W. L. 1994. Funding fundamentals: The cost/quality debate in school finance reform. 94 *Ed. Law Rep.* [9] (Dec. 1).

Coons, J. E., Clune, W., and Sugarman, S. 1969. Educational opportunity: A workable constitutional test for state financial structures. *California Law Review* 57:305.

Dayton, J. 1992. An anatomy of school funding litigation. 77 *Ed. Law Rep.* [627] (Dec. 3, 1992).

Ferguson, R. F. 1991. Paying for public education: New evidence on how and why money matters. 28 *Harv. J. Legis.* 465.

Hanushek, E. A. 1989. The impact of differential expenditures on school performance. *Educational Researcher,* 18(4):45–65.

Hawkins, A. 1991. Equity in education. 28 *Harv. J. Legis.* 565.

McCarthy, M. 1994. The courts and school finance reform. *Theory into Practice* 33(2): 89–97.

McDaniels v. Thomas, 285 S.E.2d 156 (1981).

McDuffy v. Secretary of the Executive Office of Education, 615 N.E.2d 516 (1993).

McLarin, K. J. 1994, July 23. New Jersey, denouncing local managment, prepares to take over Newark's schools. *New York Times,* p. 10.

Murnane, R. 1991. Intrepreting the evidence on *Does Money Matter?* 28 Harv. J. Legis. 457.

Murnane, R., Singer, J. D., Willet, J. B., Kemple, J. J., and Olsen, R. J. 1991. *Who will teach? Policies that matter.* Cambridge, MA: Harvard University Press.

Naapoff, A. 1994. 1993: The year of living dangerously: State courts expand the right to an education. 92 *Ed. Law Rep.* [755] (Sept. 22).

Odden, A. R. (Ed.) 1992. *Rethinking school finance: An agenda for the 1990s.* San Francisco: Jossey-Bass.

National Center for Education Statistics. 1994. *Digest of education statistics 1994.* Washington, D.C.: U.S. Dept. of Education.

National Commission on Excellence in Education. (1983). *A nation at risk: The imperatives for educational reform.* Washington, D.C.: U.S. Dept. of Education.

Robinson v. Cahill, 303 A.2d 273 (N.J. 1973).

Rose v. The Council for Better Education, Inc., 790 S.W.2d 186 (1989).

Rothstein, R. 1993, Spring. The myth of public school failure. *The American Prospect,* pp. 20 – 34.

Sadowski, M. March/April 1995. The numbers game yields simplistic answers on the link bewteen spending and outcomes. *The Harvard Education Letter,* XI(2):1 – 4.

San Antonio Independent School District v. Rodriguez, 411 U.S. 1 (1973).

Serrano v. Priest, 487 P.2d 1241 (1971).

Silber, J. 1990. *Straight shooting: What's wrong with america and how to fix it.* New York: Harper Perennial.

Slavin, R. E. 1994. After the victory: Making funding equity make a difference. *Theory into Practice* 33(2):98 – 103.

———. 1991. *The state of inequality.* Princeton, NJ: Educational Testing Service.

Sparkman, W. E. and Hartmeister, F. 1995. The Edgewood saga continues: The Texas school finance system is constitutional. *Education Law Reporter* 101(2):509 – 529.

Unrwood, J. 1989. "Changing equal protection analyses in finance equity litigation." *J. Educ. Fin.* 14:423.

Vestegen, D. A. 1994. The new wave of school finance litigation. *Phi Delta Kappan* 76(3):243 – 250.

Wise, A. 1968 *Rich schools, poor schools: The promise of equal educational opportunity.* Chicago: University of Chicago Press.

ENDNOTE

1. Living in a high property-wealthy school district not only provides a benefit to students in the way of additional educational opportunities, but the parents of the students also receive a direct benefit. Parents who live in a high wealth district do not have to expend as much effort – in the form of a tax rate – in financing their children's education as parents who reside in a property-poor school district. For

example, if School District A had an assessed valuation of $10,000,000 and School District B had an assessed valuation of $5,000,000 and both school districts wanted to raise $100,000 in revenue for their schools, District A residents would only have to assess a tax rate of $10 per $1,000 of valuation; whereas, the residents of District B would have to assess themselves $20 per $1,000 of valuation. Clearly, the residents of School District B would have to work twice as hard to raise the same amount of revenue as School District A. The disparity of unequal student benefits between high property-wealthy school districts and low property-wealthy school districts extends to unequal burdens for parents and property owners.

CHAPTER 10

Teacher Speech as a Curricular Tool: Reform Sidetracked?

Teachers must fulfill their function by precept and practice, by the very atmosphere which they generate; they must be exemplars of openmindedness and free inquiry. They cannot carry out their noble task if the conditions for the practice of a responsible and critical mind are denied to them.

— Wieman v. Updegraff, 344 U.S. 183, 196 (1952)
(J. Frankfurter, concurring)

As mentioned in the first chapter, our system of education is a creature of laws, rules, and regulations. State constitutions authorize public education. State and federal laws, school board regulations, and collective bargaining agreements define it. Since education is created by various forms of legislation, any education reform must also entail, to a large extent, legislation. We have touched upon this in our discussions of site-based management and collective bargaining, the TEIA, and charter schools.

Legislation in its various forms has attempted to initiate educational reform. But what of legislation's legal twin, litigation? Have litigation and the courts acted in concert with legislative reform, or have they been at cross-purposes with reform efforts? This chapter, which explores one example of litigation's impact on reform, highlights the question: Is litigation in battle *for* reform or *with* reform?

In Chapter 4, we noted that teachers stand at the crossroads of education. It is chiefly through their efforts that the goals of education

149

are achieved or thwarted. As Susan Moore Johnson writes: "Who teaches matters" (1990, p. xiii). The teacher is the core of our highly bureaucratized system of education. Teachers perform their duty within their classroom, both isolated and protected from other educators and outside forces. It is a "division of labor that assigns individual teachers considerable discretion in decisions whose effects are confined to their individual classrooms but affords them little voice in the larger decisions made outside those classrooms" (Shedd & Bacharach, 1991, p. xii). Once inside their classroom, teachers ostensibly have a lot of freedom to do their work. "When the classroom door closes the teacher typically has enormous latitude in deciding how to teach a lesson" (Maeroff, 1988, p. 3). One teacher remarked: "When I'm in my classroom, I know I'm in control. I can teach the way I want to teach, do what I want to do" (Lieberman & Miller, 1984, p. 14). The linchpin, then, of our system of education is the teacher in his or her classroom exercising a large amount of discretion as to how that classroom is run and how knowledge is imparted and skills taught.

In most cases, the discretion that teachers exercise in their classrooms predominantly takes the form of speech. "Classroom activities are carried out in large part by verbal interaction between students and teachers" (Ornstein, 1990, p. 537), and teachers monopolize that communication (Good and Brophy, 1987). Thus, teachers' autonomy in the classroom is directly linked to their ability to control their speech. But is that autonomy threatened?

As discussed in previous chapters, teachers and the rest of education have been subjected, since around 1983, to another era of reform. This current reform movement has been characterized as consisting of two waves. The first wave was bureaucratic and regulatory in nature. Shedd and Bacharach (1994) have identified the second wave as coalescing around three propositions: "Teachers are not (but ought to be) treated as professionals; schools are (and ought not to be) top-heavy bureaucracies; and no significant improvements can occur in America's system of public education unless schools are fundamentally restructured" (p. 1). Many reformers see increased professional autonomy as reducing bureaucratic control. The Carnegie Task Force on Teaching as a Profession (1986) states as a basic tenet of its report that the bureaucratic authority of school systems must be replaced by schools in which authority is founded on a bedrock of the professional role of the teacher. By reducing bureaucratic controls, teachers can become empowered and thus assume their necessary role of autonomous professionals.

The recent discussions on reforming education have centered around empowering teachers and moving the locus of decision making closer to its impact: the local site. This autonomy is considered an important condition for schools to flourish. Sarah Lawrence Lightfoot (1983) recognizes the importance of teacher autonomy in her study of "good" high schools. She writes: "The teachers in these schools are recognized as the critical authorities; the ones who will guide the learning, growth, and development of students. . . . They give shape to what is taught, how it is taught and in what context it is transmitted" (pp. 333 – 334). Good schools are associated with a high degree of teacher autonomy in the classroom. In a similar vein, Bernard Gifford, then Dean of the Graduate School of Education, University of California, states: "If we are to make a dent in the problems we face in public education, we're going to have to find ways of permitting talented teachers to play a much larger role. We need to find ways of giving talented people, first rate professionals, extra leverage" (Green, 1986, Preface).

A teacher's control over the classroom is structured, to a large degree, by school board policies. Boards of education are legally empowered to adopt the curriculum for their schools; they are also empowered to hire teachers to teach that adopted curriculum. As discussed before, classroom instruction is characterized by speech and teachers monopolize that speech. Instruction is the curriculum and instruction is, in large measure, teacher speech. Therefore, the school board's ability to effectively control the curriculum is largely measured by its ability to control teacher speech. But teachers' autonomy in the classroom is directly linked to their ability to control their speech.

Teacher speech as curriculum has major implications for education. It juxtaposes the community's right, through its elected board members, to determine what should be taught with a teacher's desire for an expansive view of academic freedom. Rosenholtz (1989) illuminates this tension when she writes: "In successful schools, it might be argued, the problem of professional autonomy may arise at the intersection where competing individual and communal needs collide" (p. 220). Professional autonomy can be seen as teacher classroom speech, and communal needs can be cast as the school district's articulated curriculum and educational programs.

The courts have recently been applying a standard from a student free expression case, *Hazelwood School District v. Kuhlmeier* (1988), to explicate this intersection of teacher in-class speech and curriculum — autonomy and control. Two recent court cases involving teacher classroom speech, *Miles v. Denver Public Schools* (1991) and *Ward v. Hickey* (1993), used *Hazelwood* to define teacher speech as curriculum, thus limiting professional autonomy. This chapter will focus on teacher classroom speech as curriculum and its impact on teacher autonomy by analyzing *Miles* and *Ward* in the context of the *Hazelwood* rationale applied to teacher in class comments. But first we will review *Hazelwood* to establish a firm background for the discussion.

HAZELWOOD SCHOOL DISTRICT v. KUHLMEIER: SCHOOLS MAY REGULATE SCHOOL-SPONSORED SPEECH BASED ON A LEGITIMATE PEDAGOGICAL CONCERN

In *Hazelwood,* student contributors to a school newspaper published as part of a journalism class contested their principal's decision to delete two pages from the newspaper prior to publication. The principal based his action on a fear that the students quoted in two articles on teenage pregnancy and divorce could be identified.

The case eventually wound its way to the United States Supreme Court, which, in 1988, upheld the principal's action. The High Court decided that public schools need only tolerate a student's private expression; the school is not required to promote it. Speech, or conduct, that the public could reasonably believe carried the imprimatur of the school could be controlled by the school. The school need not lend its name to anybody who wants to appropriate it for personal use. The decision also suggests that the area that is most easily identified with a school, and consequently under the greatest control of the school, is its curriculum.

The Court began its analysis by asking whether the school constituted a public forum, where all manner of speech must be allowed. If the school had not been opened for indiscriminate use by the general public, then the school was not considered a public forum. If the school is not a public forum, then "school officials may impose reasonable restrictions on the speech of students, teachers, and other members of the school community" (*Hazelwood,* 1988, p. 267). After determining that the student newspaper was not a public forum, the Court focused on whether the students' expression was school-sponsored. The *Hazelwood* court

---

THE PUBLIC FORUM

A public forum is an arena reserved for the greatest protection of free speech.

- "Wherever the title of streets and parks may rest, they have immemorially been held in trust for the use of the public and, time out of mind, have been used for purposes of assembly, communicating thoughts between citizens, and discussing public questions"—Hague v. CIO, 307 U.S. 496 (1939).
- When the state, or a state agency, has established a public forum, the state may regulate the speech that takes place in that forum only through "regulations of time, place, and manner of expression which are content-neutral, are narrowly tailored to serve a significant governmental interest, and leave open ample alternative channels of communication"—United States Postal Service v. Council of Greenburgh Civic Associations, 453 U.S. 114 (1981).
- However, since classrooms are not considered public forums, the state may more easily regulate the speech that takes place within the classroom. "In addition to time, place, and manner regulations, the state may reserve the forum for its intended purposes, communicative or otherwise, as long as the regulation on speech is reasonable and not an effort to suppress expression merely because public officials oppose the speaker's view"—Id. at 131, n. 7.

---

found that the school had authority over such school-sponsored publications as theatrical productions and "other expressive activities that students, parents, and other members of the public might reasonably perceive to bear the imprimatur of the school" (p. 271). The Supreme Court held that educators do not offend the Constitution by exercising editorial control over school-sponsored expression "so long as their actions are reasonably related to legitimate pedagogical concerns" (p. 273).

By permitting schools to regulate school-sponsored expression based on reasonable pedagogical concerns, the court was clearly giving deference to the school authorities in curricular matters. Under the *Hazelwood* guidelines, school authorities may exercise extensive control over speech that is part of the curriculum, especially if the public believes that the speech represents the school's position. The decision has important implications for teachers if their speech is considered part of the curriculum, a view that *Hazelwood* clearly supports. We will next review an application of *Hazelwood* to teacher speech.

MILES v. DENVER PUBLIC SCHOOLS: TEACHER SPEECH AS CURRICULUM

John G. Miles was employed by the Denver Public Schools and taught at Thomas Jefferson High School. On March 31, 1989, while conducting his ninth-grade government class, a student asked him to explain the difference between the present high school and the high school of past years. Miles responded that the school was not as clean as it had been in years past and that school discipline had been better in the past. He went on to state, "I don't think in 1967 you would have seen two students making out on the tennis court." He then specifically named one of the two students involved in a recent alleged tennis court rendezvous. At the time Miles commented, the tennis court incident was the topic of conversation throughout the school. According to rumor, two students had engaged in sexual intercourse on the tennis court during lunchtime. Miles was not a witness to the incident and heard of the incident from a colleague who had heard of it from two students claiming to have witnessed it. Miles never sought official confirmation of the rumor before repeating it in class.

The students allegedly involved in the tennis court incident and their parents complained to school officials about Miles's statement in class. Following meetings with Miles and several other individuals, the school administration placed Miles on paid administrative leave for four days while the school district conducted an investigation. Miles wrote to the principal apologizing for exercising "bad judgment." At the conclusion of the investigation, Miles was issued a letter of reprimand and placed on paid administrative leave.

Eight months after Miles was sanctioned, he filed a lawsuit claiming that the imposition of paid administrative leave and the placement of the letter of reprimand in his personnel file violated his free speech rights.

In trial court proceedings, Miles claimed that his answer to the student's question was protected by his right to free speech. In order to prevail with this argument, he was required to satisfy a test articulated by the United States Supreme Court regarding the free speech rights of

---

TEACHER'S FREE SPEECH

Courts use a three-step analysis to determine whether a school district has abridged a teacher's right to free speech.

1. The plaintiff must demonstrate that his or her conduct was protected.
   A. The speech must be on a matter of public concern—Connick v. Myers 461 U.S. 138 (1983).
   B. The interest of the employee in speaking must outweigh the interest of the state in promoting the efficiency of the public service it performs through its employees—Pickering v. Board of Education 391 U.S. 563 (1968). The *Pickering* balancing test considers such issues as harmony in the workplace, harm to a close working relationship, and detriment to an employee's work performance.
2. The plaintiff must demonstrate that such protected activity was a substantial or motivating factor in the adverse employment decision.
3. If one and two are established, the employer may show that the employment action would have been taken even in the absence of the protected conduct—Mt. Healthy City School District Board of Education v. Doyle 429 U.S. 274 (1977).

---

public employees. This test required Miles to show that (1) the speech for which he was disciplined was constitutionally protected and (2) the protected speech motivated the employment decision. According to the Supreme Court's test, once Miles had made these showings, the school district then had the burden of showing by a preponderance of the evidence that it would have made the same disciplinary decision absent the protected speech.

The district court, in viewing the first prong of the analysis had to determine if Miles's answer to the student's question (1) constituted a matter of public concern and (2) whether Miles's interest in answering as he did outweighed the school district's interest, as a public employer, in promoting the efficiency of the public service it performs through its employees.

The court found that Miles's answer pertained to the affairs of his students and that his answer was not motivated solely by personal interest. The answer was ''calculated to enlighten students to the relative condition of the institution in which he instructed and in which the students were enrolled. . . . Thus, the topic itself was a matter of public concern'' (*Miles*, 1990, p. 1412).

It appeared that Miles had cleared his first hurdle, but the court continued its analysis. The court proceeded to analyze the statement itself and found that Miles was not reprimanded for making the now-and-then comparison, but rather, he was reprimanded for discussing the rumored incident on the tennis court and for revealing the name of one of the students allegedly involved in the incident. The court found that revealing the name of a student did not address a matter of public concern. Thus Miles's argument that his status as a teacher heightened his First Amendment interest failed. Germane to our discussion about the role of teacher speech in the classroom, the court concluded that: ''By the very nature of the teaching profession, poor judgment will most likely manifest itself in instructor's speech'' (*Miles*, 1990, p. 1413). Having lost at the district court, Miles appealed.

The court of appeals began its analysis of the case in the same basic fashion as the lower court. Just as the lower court had done, the appellate court laid out the three-part test for determining the free speech rights of public employees. But the court of appeals quickly departed from the district court's analysis. Instead of applying one Supreme Court case to determine whether Miles's speech was a matter of public concern, the court of appeals looked to another Supreme Court decision for guidance on whether Miles's speech was constitutionally protected—*Hazelwood School District v. Kuhlmeier.*

Just as in *Hazelwood*, where the Supreme Court determined whether a school newspaper constituted a public forum, the court of appeals in *Miles* considered whether Miles's ninth-grade classroom was a public forum. As we have discussed, a traditional public forum would be a street corner or a park.

In the appellate court's view, Miles's classroom was quite different from a traditional public forum, such as a street corner. ''A podium before a captive audience of public school children is decisively different from a street corner,'' the court observed (*Miles*, 1991, p. 776). Instead, Miles's classroom was more akin to the school newspaper in *Hazelwood*, which the Supreme Court had determined was not a public forum. Following *Hazelwood's* guidance, the *Miles* court concluded that the school had reserved Miles's classroom for a particular purpose, teaching government, and not as a public forum for any discussion that the teacher might choose to lead.

As in *Hazelwood*, the court next turned to the question of whether

Miles's expression during the ninth-grade government class was school-sponsored. The court concluded that "if students' expression in a school newspaper bears the imprimatur of the school, then a teacher's expression in the 'traditional classroom setting' also bears the imprimatur of the school" (*Miles,* 1991, p. 776). Since the court found that Miles's speech to his class was school-sponsored and took place in a nonpublic forum, it applied the Hazelwood standard for evaluating the actions of school officials related to the regulation of school-sponsored speech.

This line of reasoning is extremely important. It has been well settled that what is taught (curriculum) is within the purview and control of the school authorities. How it is taught has generally been left to the discretion of the teacher unless the method has been clearly proscribed by the school board or it creates a material and substantial disruption.[1] The *Miles* line of reasoning contradicted this view when it ruled that a teacher's speech in the classroom is a school-sponsored speech subject — in essence merely an extension of the curriculum. This reasoning brought teacher speech under the control of school authorities and introduced administrator control into what was once largely the domain of teacher autonomy.

But what happened to the constitutional analysis that the lower court had conducted on the *Miles* fact pattern? What happened to the test that asks whether a public employee's expression addresses a matter of public concern and then balances that employee's interest in making the statement with the interest of the government, as an employer, in promoting the efficiency of the public service it performs? The court of appeals, in a very interesting argument, stated that the balancing test accounts for the state's interest as an employer, but "it does not address the significant interests of the state as educator" (*Miles,* 1991, p. 777). According to the court of appeals, the peculiar responsibilities the state bears in providing educational services within the school environment warrants the application of the *Hazelwood* standard for reviewing the regulation of classroom speech. Because the "classroom environment is *suis generis*," the court distinguished between "teacher's classroom expression and teacher's expression in other situations that would not reasonably be perceived as school-sponsored" (*Miles,* 1991, p. 777). Even though *Hazelwood* involved student expression in a secondary school and *Miles* involved a teacher's classroom expression, the court found no reason to distinguish between students and teachers where classroom discussions are concerned. For both students and teachers, in-class speech can be regulated by a school if it can show a legitimate pedagogical concern.

By focusing on the school district's role as educator, rather than employer, the *Miles* court reduced the classroom teacher to an education tool, much like the curriculum. Since the school has great latitude in determining the curriculum, this development may have greatly curtailed a teacher's constitutional right to free expression when the speech takes place in the classroom. If so, what happens to teacher autonomy when teacher speech can be controlled by school authorities much like curriculum can be controlled?

John Miles's experience suggests the answer to this question. Because his classroom comments were considered school-sponsored, the school authorities were permitted to restrain his comments based on what the court found to be a legitimate pedagogical interest. Since the court found that Miles's particular comments were not constitutionally protected, the court did not have to balance Miles's free speech rights with the school district's interests as public employer. The imposition of administrative leave and the letter of reprimand did not violate Miles's constitutional rights.

The court of appeals did not distinguish between students and teachers where classroom speech was the issue. The interests of the state as educator gave the school wide latitude in regulating classroom speech, even if that speech came from a teacher. In effect, administrative control increased at the expense of teacher autonomy through a rationale developed within the context of a student speech case. What was devised for students, whose constitutional rights are not co-extensive with adults, was cut whole cloth to fit teachers.

But *Miles* is not the only case in which a court has applied *Hazelwood's* reasoning to a teacher's classroom speech. Another example of *Hazelwood's* long reach is found in *Ward v. Hickey*.

WARD v. HICKEY: MUST SCHOOLS GIVE PRIOR NOTICE OF WHAT KIND OF CLASSROOM SPEECH IS PUNISHABLE?

Toby Klang Ward was hired on an annual basis for three consecutive years starting in 1979. Ward taught biology at Belmont High School in Massachusetts. In June of 1982, the Belmont School Committee voted not to reappoint Ward, thus denying her tenure. Ward brought suit in federal court against the three board members who voted against her, alleging that the nonrenewal violated her First Amendment right to free speech. Specifically, Ward alleged that her nonrenewal was in retaliation for comments she made in her ninth-grade biology class concerning the abortion of Down's Syndrome fetuses. She sought injunctive, declaratory, and compensatory relief.

This case wound its way to the First Circuit Court of Appeals by starting with a magistrate's recommendations, which were accepted by the federal district court. On the issues most germane to our discussion, the court found that free speech does not grant teachers a license to say or write in class whatever they may feel like. While the court found that the plaintiff had no clearly established right to discuss certain controversial subjects in her high school classroom, she did enjoy a constitutional right to notice concerning what conduct could form the basis of an adverse employment decision. Ward's original complaint was defective because it did not contain allegations that the defendants failed to give her notice that discussing such topics as abortion and Down's Syndrome was impermissible. Accordingly, the court gave Ward leave to amend her complaint, which ultimately led to her undoing. She lost when the court entered a judgment in favor of the defendants. Ward appealed.

The court of appeals found that the district court's reliance on a forum analysis for viewpoint discrimination was flawed. Instead, the court concluded that the *Hazelwood* rationale was the appropriate standard. The reason the court of appeals rejected the forum analysis was that the school committee could violate viewpoint neutrality in a classroom setting involving teacher speech. In other words, the school board, when viewing speech that takes place within a classroom, need not view the content of the speech in a neutral manner. The board can disagree with the content of the speech and take action to stop it. Speech can be stopped or punished because of the message's content, not just for the effect the message could have toward creating a material and substantial disruption.

Relying on *Hazelwood,* the court of appeals asserted that the school authorities are entitled to greater deference in regulating school-sponsored speech and that the curriculum was obviously school-sponsored.

"Like the newspaper [in *Hazelwood*], a teacher's speech in the class-room is part of the curriculum" (*Ward,* 1993, p. 453). If a teacher's speech in the classroom is part of the curriculum, school authorities may reasonably limit a teacher's speech in that setting, and the restriction need not be viewpoint neutral. In fact, the restriction would need to further a clear viewpoint, a legitimate pedagogical concern articulated by the school board.

The court set out a two-part test for ascertaining the constitutionality of a regulation of teacher classroom speech: (1) the regulation must be reasonably related to a legitimate pedagogical concern, and (2) notice of what conduct is prohibited must be provided to the teacher. The first prong of the test depends on, among other things, the age and sophistication of the students, the relationship between the teaching method and a valid educational objective, and the context and manner of the presentation. The second prong – notice – need not be so specific that school authorities must expressly prohibit every imaginable inappropriate conduct by teachers. According to the court, the relevant inquiry is: "Based on existing regulations, policies, discussions, and other forms of communi-cation between school administrators and teachers, was it reasonable for the school to expect the teacher to know that [his/]her conduct was prohibited?" (*Ward,* 1993, p. 454). As with *Miles,* the First Circuit afforded school authorities great deference in regulating teacher class-room speech.

But what about Toby Klang Ward? She lost, perhaps because she failed to address the issue of notice at trial court level. Because of this over-sight, we do not know whether Ward might have won on the issue of inadequate notice, nor do we know specifically what constitutes proper notice in the appellate court's view.

TEACHER AUTONOMY: A CONCLUDING POSTSCRIPT

This discussion started by pointing out that teachers have enjoyed a certain measure of autonomy in the classroom. The current wave of school reform seeks to buttress and strengthen that autonomy through professionalizing the ranks of teachers. Many reformers have lined up behind this argument. Have the courts joined the line, or are they going in a different direction?

Prior to *Hazelwood,* while teachers did not have an unfettered right to say anything they wanted in class, the school district carried the burden of proving that their actions aimed at curtailing or punishing teacher in-class speech were warranted. That burden often was difficult to shoulder. The post-*Hazelwood* landscape has surely lightened that load. The concept of teacher classroom speech being school-sponsored speech clearly indicates that the legitimate pedagogical interest is the school district's and not the teacher's. According to the analysis conducted in *Miles,* the only pedagogical interest that was reviewed was the school's. There was no inquiry into whether Miles was pursuing an appropriate educational purpose. In a *Hazelwood* analysis, the school district must first articulate a legitimate pedagogical reason to support its action, and then the teacher must demonstrate that the activity in dispute is consistent with that legitimate pedagogical concern. Clearly, if a teacher's speech must conform to the legitimate pedagogical interests of the school district, a teacher's classroom autonomy is diminished. The rebuttable presumption of correct behavior would no longer lie with the teacher.

Moreover, there is the possibility that a district will not have to articulate its pedagogical interest prior to imposing a penalty for teacher speech. In *Miles,* after all, the principal articulated the school district's pedagogical interest as part of the discipline and without prior warning. On possibly a more positive note, *Ward* provides some requirement of notice of prohibited conduct. *Ward* also provides some guidance about the necessary relationship between the teacher's contested speech and a legitimate pedagogical concern.

The application of the *Hazelwood* standard to teacher speech in the classroom bears close watching. A judicial pattern that accepts this standard may signal that teacher autonomy is an endangered concept and that a teacher's classroom speech can be monitored by school authorities and regulated like any other part of the curriculum. A teacher's voice may come to be seen as merely a canned recording that can be turned off and on at will or discarded for another voice if it conflicts with the authorities' wishes. If that happens, a teacher's classroom autonomy, which many educational leaders say is so important for reform, may give way before judicial deference to school authority.

Reform efforts may be going in one direction—emphasizing teacher autonomy and professionalism—while the courts move in the opposite direction toward greater control of teachers, teaching methods, and the curriculum. In other words, the courts may not be battling for reform, but rather against reform. *Hazelwood,* in particular, may have breached the fragile wall of academic freedom in public schools by taking control of classroom speech from teachers and giving it to school boards. School boards may be emboldened to rush through this breach to control the professional judgment of teachers. If so, this impulse must be checked. Reform calls for a strengthening of professional autonomy, not a weakening of this positive force. School board members act like back-seat drivers when they second-guess the decisions of classroom teachers. And though their interferences may not wreck the car, they can certainly annoy and distract the driver.

REFERENCES

Carnegie Task Force on Teaching as a Profession. (1986). *A nation prepared: Teachers for the 21st century.* New York: Carnegie Forum on Education and the Economy.

Good, T. L. and Brophy, J. E. (1987). *Looking in classrooms,* fourth edition. New York: Harper & Row.

Green, J. (Ed.) (1986). *What next? More leverage for teachers.* Denver, CO: Education Commission of the States.

Hazelwood School District v. Kuhlmeier, 484 U.S. 260 (1988).

Johnson, S. M. (1990). *Teachers at work: Achieving success in our schools.* New York: Basic Books.

Lieberman, A. and Miller, L. (1984). *Teachers, their world, and their work.* Alexandria, VA: Association for Supervision and Curriculum Development.

Lightfoot, S. L. (1983). *The good high school: Portraits of character and culture.* New York: Basic Books.

Maeroff, G. I. (1988). *The empowerment of teachers: Overcoming the crisis of confidence.* New York: Teachers College Press.

Miles v. Denver Public Schools, 733 F. Supp. 1410 (D. Colo. 1990).

Miles v. Denver Public Schools, 944 F.2d 773 (10th Cir. 1991).

Ornstein, A. C. (1990). *Strategies for effective teaching.* New York: Harper Collins.

Rosenholtz, S. J. (1989). *Teachers' workplace: The social organization of schools.* New York: Longman.

Shedd, J. B. and Bacharach, S. B. (1991). *Tangled hierarchies: Teachers as professionals and the management of schools.* San Francisco: Jossey-Bass.

Ward v. Hickey, 996 F.2d 448 (1st Cir. 1993).

ENDNOTE

1. See, for example, Parducci v. Rutland, 316 F. Supp. 352 (N.D. Ala. 1970), where a school district violated a teacher's right to academic freedom when she was dismissed for assigning her eleventh-grade class a satire by Kurt Vonnegut Jr. after she was

advised not to teach the story again. The court found that the school board had failed to demonstrate that the assignment was inappropriate reading for high school juniors or that it created a material and substantial disruption. Also, see Keefe v. Geanakos, 418 F. 2d 359 (1st Cir. 1969), where a teacher's use of a recent issue of the *Atlantic Monthly* magazine contained an article that used the term *motherfucker* a number of times was protected. The court found a substantive right of a teacher to choose a teaching method that serves a demonstrated educational purpose and a procedural right not to be discharged for the use of a teaching method not prohibited by clear regulation.

CHAPTER 11

The Unkept Promise of Brown v. Board of Education: *How Can Its Vision Be Fulfilled?*†

> *Over the years, the purpose of school desegregation has become so obfuscated that many have forgotten this simple fact: Litigation for desegregation was undertaken because Blacks wanted better educational opportunities for their children.*
>
> —Charles Vert Willie (1988)

BACKGROUND

Forty years after the Supreme Court's decision in *Brown v. Board of Education,* it is impossible to shut our eyes to this simple revelation: something has gone horribly wrong. In spite of the fact that the majesty of the U.S. Constitution was invoked to stop racial segregation in the nation's schools and in spite of massive judicial intervention and long-term court supervision of U.S. school districts, the educational experience of many African American children is deteriorating, especially in the nation's inner-city school districts and the schools of the rural South.

The evidence is all around us, and it is overwhelming. First, any assessment of racial distribution in the nation's schools—particularly our inner-city schools—shows quite clearly that desegregation is often a fiction. In the large urban districts, student populations continue to be heavily dominated by African Americans and Hispanics. In 1986–1987,

†This chapter is authored by Kofi Lomotey and Richard Fossey.

the twenty-five largest metropolitan districts enrolled almost 30 percent of the nation's African American students and Hispanic students, but only about 3 percent of the nation's white students (Orfield & Monfort, 1988). In many urban districts—Chicago, Cleveland, Detroit, New Orleans, Philadelphia, and Washington, D.C., to name a few—a majority of the students are African American. In other districts, the student body is predominantly Hispanic. This is true, not only in such southern school districts as Dade County, Florida, and San Antonio, but in many northern school districts as well. During 1988–1989, more than 40 percent of the nation's African American and Hispanic students were enrolled in the 100 largest school districts (National Center for Educational Statistics, 1991, p. 4). During 1993, these groups comprised at least 76 percent of the student enrollment in nine of the ten largest school districts (National Center for Educational Statistics, 1994).

Forty years after *Brown v. Board of Education,* African American and Hispanic students are often still segregated in predominantly African American and Hispanic schools. During the 1988-1989 school year, roughly a quarter of the nation's African American and Hispanic students attended schools that were less than 5 percent white (Tye, 1991). In the five largest U.S. districts, the school populations in a majority of the school sites is at least 80 percent African American and Hispanic (National Center for Educational Statistics, 1991).

Northeastern schools are the most segregated schools in the country for African American students. In 1988–1989, more than 40 percent of the region's African American students were enrolled in schools that were less than 5 percent white. Ironically, the least segregated part of the country is the South, although recent studies show a trend of increasing racial isolation for southern African American students (Eaton, 1994). Moreover, some of the strategies adopted to encourage desegregation may have had an opposite effect.

For example, some urban districts adopted school choice plans as a strategy for achieving desegregation. The proponents of these plans (sometimes called "magnet schools" or "options") argued that students from diverse racial or socioeconomic backgrounds could be enticed to a previously racially isolated school if the school embodied a distinctive educational philosophy or offered a specialized educational program.

In 1990, Donald Moore and Suzanne Davenport published a study on school option or school choice programs in which they concluded that these programs were not a good strategy for racial desegregation. On the contrary, the programs often had a tendency to stratify urban students by race. Selective vocational, magnet, and examination high schools tended to have a high percentage of white students compared with their overall enrollment in the school district. Nonselective, low-income and low-to-moderate-income schools typically admitted a high percentage of African American and Hispanic students (Moore & Davenport, 1990).

Moore and Davenport's study contributes to a growing body of evidence showing that some of the most popular strategies for desegregating schools have been unsuccessful (Singletary, 1992). Indeed, for Hispanic students, schools are becoming more segregated, not less. In 1968–1969, 23.1 percent of Hispanic students attended schools that were no more than 10 percent white. In 1984–1985, the comparable figure was 31 percent (Orfield & Monfort, 1988, p. 19). During the 1986–1987 school year, 50.2 percent of the Hispanic students in the Chicago school district attended schools that were 99–100 percent African American and Hispanic. In Houston, 53 percent of Hispanic students were in intensely segregated schools; in San Antonio, 75 percent; and in New York City, 68 percent.

Second, by a variety of standards, African American students are not doing well in the nation's schools. Dropout rates, suspension rates, and special education participation rates are high among African American students and higher than for European American students (e.g., Kennedy, 1993).

Although the National Center for Education Statistics (1994) reported that the dropout rate for African Americans is going down, this trend masks the stark reality of extremely high dropout rates in many urban districts. For example, in Philadelphia, where 63 percent of the student enrollment is African American, only half of a class of ninth graders graduate in four years (Celis, 1995). In many of the urban districts of New Jersey, the on-time high school completion rate for African American males is 50 percent or below (Burch, 1992). In New Orleans, where 89 percent of the student body is African American, 55 percent of a cohort of ninth graders failed to graduate on time in 1993 (Fossey & Garvin, 1995).

Not only are African Americans and Hispanic Americans more likely to drop out of school than white students, they are more likely to be placed in special education, where many fail to thrive. During the 1986–1987 school year, African American and Hispanic American students comprised 30 percent of the school-age population, but they comprised 35 percent of the students classified as seriously emotionally disturbed (SED), 40 percent classified as trainable mentally retarded (TMR), and 42 percent classified as educable mentally retarded (EMR) (Gartner & Lipsky, 1989).

For African American students, their disproportionate representation in special education is especially stark. African Americans were only 16 percent of the total school enrollment in 1986 – 1987, but they comprised 35 percent of the EMR students, 27 percent of the TMR students, and 27 percent of the SED students (Gartner & Lipsky, 1989). According to some studies, African American children are twice as likely to be placed in some category of special education as white children (Richardson, 1994).

Suspension and expulsion rates are also higher for African American students than for white students and far higher for African American males. A study of suspensions and expulsions in Louisiana schools during 1991 – 1992 found that 41 percent of all suspensions and 58 percent of all expulsions were African American males, even though they only comprised 22 percent of the school population. African American females constituted 21 percent of the school population and 19 percent of the students expelled, while white female students, comprising 25 percent of school enrollment, accounted for only 3 percent of total expulsions (Kennedy, 1993).

Third, if the purpose of education is to enable our young people to earn a decent living and take their place in the nation's civic and political life, then surely the *Brown* experiment has so far been a failure for African American youth. Although the gap in achievement levels between whites and African Americans and Hispanic Americans decreased between 1977 and 1990, white children still outperform African American and Hispanic American youth at all age levels and in all subjects. One study analyzed school records of African American and Mexican American students and discovered that these students consistently performed below average (Ogbu, 1986). Although African American children seem to start their educational lives with cognitive, sensory, and motor skills equal to their European classmates, their academic performance seems to decrease the longer they stay in school (Parham & Parham, 1989). According to Stanfield (1982), "Even in schools where the racial gap in achievement is closing, there are still extensive racial resegregation patterns" (p. 90).

Moreover, if *Brown v. Board of Education* had improved educational opportunities for African Americans, we would expect to see improvements in African Americans' economic status. A recent U.S. Census Bureau report indicates, however, that more African American families, not less, have been sinking below the poverty line in recent years. Thirty-one percent of African American families with children lived in poverty in 1993, up from 28 percent in 1969 (Bennett, 1995). According to the same report, African American children are three times as likely as white children to live in poverty (Bennett, 1995).

WHY HAS COURT-ORDERED DESEGREGATION FAILED?

Why has court-ordered desegregation failed to benefit African American children? First, after *Brown v. Board of Education* was decided by the Supreme Court, desegregation litigation gradually shifted from an effort to provide equal educational opportunities for African Americans to a political struggle for power and resources among school districts, state government, and other educational elites. As Gary Orfield (Feldman et al., 1994, p. 5) pointed out in the foreword to a review of desegregation:

> The plaintiffs often seemed to be almost irrelevant. They were not consulted seriously about the remedy, they did not evaluate whether or not the minority children and communities actually benefited, and the remedies were terminated without plaintiff agreement that constitutional obligations had been fulfilled. What was presented as a remedy of the harms of segregation typically did not identify those harms and did not measure whether they were cured. In the court ordered cases, the remedies were basically a result of a political battle between school districts who were trying to get as much money as possible for their favorite programs and the state governments who were trying to spend as little as possible for as few years as possible. The victims of segregation often seemed lost in the shuffle. (p. 5)

To a certain extent, the civil rights lawyers who brought desegregation lawsuits were slow to realize that improving the condition of African American children involved far more than placing them in classrooms with white children. As Bell (1983) observed:

> Had we civil rights lawyers been more attuned to the primary goal of African American parents—the effective schooling of their children—and less committed to the attainment of our ideal—racially integrated schools—we might have recognized sooner that merely integrating

schools, in a society still committed to white dominance, would not insure our clients and their children the equal educational opportunity for which they have sacrificed so much and waited so long. (p. 575)

In other words, in the struggle to desegregate the nation's schools, the means got substituted for the ends. Desegregation was intended to be a tool to bring about equal educational opportunities for African Americans, but school leaders, courts, and lawyers lost sight of that fact. Instead, they focused on such things as racial balance in districts and schools, white flight, and districtwide test scores. School leaders considered desegregation to be a success if they could say that white flight was limited, opposition to busing was muted, or the percentage of various racial groups was a mirror reflection of the larger community. None of these success measures dealt with the fundamental issue—improving the academic achievement and life chances of African Americans.

Second, in the aftermath of *Brown,* we failed to develop new pedagogies. Although the courts were able to require white and African American students to be educated in physical proximity to one another, they were unable to mandate that schools compensate for more subtle forms of exclusion that African American children encounter in the classroom (Graham, 1993). Today, segregated schools have been replaced by other exclusionary measures, including tracking; a declining number of African American teachers; degrading euphemisms; a pseudoscience of mental measurement; explosion in special education enrollments, suspensions, and expulsions of African Americans; cosmetic curricular changes; and, in many urban schools, de facto resegregation (Hilliard, 1988).

Third, we failed to change the attitudes and values of many of the people who staffed our previously segregated schools. When school desegregation was first implemented, many teachers and administrators were not prepared to deal with such a change, and many resisted vehemently. Some teachers left school districts, retired, or left the profession altogether in order not to have to deal with desegregation.

As Dempsey and Noblit (1993) indicate, even many of the policymakers acted ''ignorant'' of the fact that desegregation made life harder for African Americans than for European Americans. Frequently, it was African American students, not white children, who were bused to promote desegregation. When desegregation plans required schools to be closed, the buildings targeted for closure were often ones that were located in African American neighborhoods.

Moreover, cumbersome transfer and hiring rules, advocated by teachers' unions and designed to protect senior teachers, were largely left in place after *Brown*. As a result, it was often extremely difficult for schools to respond flexibly to changing school conditions. For example, a recent study of the Boston Schools, where 48 percent of the student population is African American, revealed that the pupil/teacher ratio was quite low—only 13 to 1. However, complex work rules and collective bargaining provisions prevented the district from organizing its teachers in such a way as to take full advantage of its relatively large teaching staff (Miles, 1993). Murnane and colleagues (1991) have pointed out that complex transfer rules also hinder school districts from recruiting good teachers.

Nor did *Brown* have any effect on a disputatious collective bargaining process that often prevents educators from working together in a collegial manner. Indeed, in some districts, adversarial labor relations have largely negated such school reform initiatives as shared decision making or site-based management—initiatives that were designed to build trust and cooperation between teachers and administrators (Fossey, 1993; Fossey & Miles, 1992). Unfortunately, the districts where labor relations are often the most contentious are inner-city districts, the very districts where large numbers of African American and Hispanic American children attend school.

Often, basic reforms—abolition of corporal punishment, for example—were neglected while districts pursued superficial "restructuring" initiatives. Despite the fact that there has been a nationwide flurry of school reform legislation, more than twenty states still permit school staff members to inflict physical punishment on children. Furthermore, studies have shown that African American children are the victims of this form of punishment in disproportionate numbers (Hyman, 1990, p. 57).

For example, the East Baton Rouge Parish School District, an urban district with a predominantly African American student body, has expended substantial resources and much rhetoric on school "redesign," supposedly to develop better learning environments for the children of the parish—both African American and white. Nevertheless, the district continues to practice corporal punishment and issues standardized wooden paddles from warehouses to the district's principals (*Advocate* staff, 1995; Beck, 1995).

In addition, although *Brown* was able to bring African American and white children into closer proximity with one another, it was unable to assure that African American children would attend school in safe and secure environments. African American children frequently attend schools and live in neighborhoods that are violent environments. Too often, school administrators take a casual attitude toward children's safety, as evidenced by the common practice of covering up child sexual abuse by school employees (Stein, 1993). In many school settings, African Americans find that their primary value to school authorities derives from their athletic talents, not their intellectual potential or their intrinsic human worth (Bissinger, 1990).

Fourth, a number of urban districts with predominantly African American student bodies are plagued by mismanagement or outright corruption—a sure sign that the care and well-being of students are being neglected. For example, in 1993, records of asbestos inspections in New York City schools were found to have been falsified (Marks, 1993). At about the same time, an investigative report was issued that described fraud and corruption by some New York City school custodians (Flamm et al., 1992; Sack, 1993). Meanwhile, in Washington, D.C., school authorities allegedly overstated the district's enrollment by several thousand students (Schmidt, 1995), and during one fifteen-month period, District of Columbia school officials hired over 100 school employees with criminal records (Report: DC schools employ hundreds, 1995). The Chicago and New York school districts have found it necessary to appoint full-time investigators to deal with fraud, waste, and mismanagement (Bradley, 1994; Schmidt, 1993).

Fifth, school desegregation efforts have failed because we have not confronted the unequal power relations in society and schools. Nor have issues of power been addressed. Power is the ability to define reality, to convince others that it is their reality, and to convince those others to act in accordance with that defined reality. U.S. society is socially stratified based upon racism, classism, and other forms of illegitimate exclusion (Stanfield, 1982). Schools, of course, are a microcosm of the larger society, and accordingly, they perpetuate these "isms." Racial and other inequities have not been addressed in society or in the schools (Obgu, 1986).

In short, *Brown v. Board of Education* failed to achieve its promise because we lost sight of the original goal—improving the lives of African American children—and because we failed to make fundamental changes in school leadership, pedagogy, school culture, and power relationships. Instead, the institutions and educators that our society assigned to educate African American children made few adjustments for the benefit of these children. For the schools to provide African American children with equal educational opportunities — which is what *Brown* guarantees — we must rededicate ourselves to transforming U.S. schools into places that nurture and respect all children.

WHAT NEEDS TO BE DONE?

If we are serious about improving the academic, social, and cultural outlook of African American students, we need to begin by forgetting about school integration. While the notion of all students going to school together may seem ideal, it is not the solution to the critical problem of the persistent and pervasive disenfranchisement of African Americans. We need to begin to focus — directly — on the academic, social, and cultural success of African American students — *wherever they may be attending school.*

Pedagogy

First, for the promise of *Brown v. Board of Education* to be fulfilled, U.S. schools must embrace a culturally equitable pedagogy. Such a pedagogy includes at least three concepts: (1) the development of culturally diverse role models in the curriculum; (2) understanding, appreciation, and respect of cultural differences; and (3) a reconsideration of traditional Eurocentric worldviews.

Gloria Ladson-Billings (1994) has pointed out that a culturally equitable education requires culturally relevant teaching. In essence, she argues that curricular change is not sufficient; we need to change the way we look at the world and the way we act, and ultimately, we need to change the power relationships within the classroom and within U.S. society. Ladson-Billings outlines six tenets of culturally relevant teaching.

(1) Students whose educational, economic, political, and cultural futures are most tenuous are helped to become intellectual leaders in the classroom.

(2) Students are apprenticed in a learning community, rather than taught in an isolated and unrelated way.

(3) Students' real-life experiences are legitimized as they become part of the "official" curriculum.

(4) Teachers and students participate in a broad conception of literacy that incorporates both literature and oratory.

(5) Teachers and students engage in a collective struggle against the status quo.

(6) Teachers are cognizant of themselves as political beings.

All students need role models in the schools that look like them. Students need to be able to ''see themselves in the curriculum'' (Lomotey, 1989). This entails seeing some teachers and administrators who look like them, seeing some people in textbooks who look like them and seeing pictures of people on their classroom walls who look like them. We must increase the number of minority teachers and administrators that both minority and majority students see in their schools. This serves as a daily symbol of the fact that power and expertise are shared and are not the exclusive domain of one group. Adult role models of both races working together in an educational environment is a powerful statement to both white and minority students. In addition, students need to be exposed to a curriculum that reflects their culture and history.

Understanding, appreciation, and respect for cultural differences speaks to the way in which we prepare teachers to teach. More often than not, teachers are only prepared to teach a particular type of child with a particular set of habits, values, and cultural characteristics. The dilemma is that most children in U.S. schools do not fit a general mold. The result is that teachers—unprepared to deal with cultural differences—often do whatever is necessary to remove perceived ''obstructions'' so they can go on teaching the particular type of child they are prepared to teach. Other children are: (a) placed in the back of the room, never to be heard from again; (b) sent to the principal's office for subsequent suspension or expulsion; or (c) recommended for special education. Simply put, we are not preparing teachers for the cultural differences that children bring to the classroom, and this accounts for at least part of the reason that African American children are suspended, expelled, placed in special education, or otherwise ''pushed out'' of the nation's classrooms in disproportionate numbers.

These cultural differences are reflected in values, in language, dress, and learning styles. For example, consider the following. If a French-speaking child is asked to repeat the phrase ''the man,'' because of the absence of the ''th'' sound in the French language, the child will typically say ''ze man.'' The teacher's response will likely be positive—an acknowledgment that the child is ''cultured'' and bilingual. On the other hand, if an

African American child is given the same phrase, the child will typically say "da man." There is no "th" sound in most west African languages, and the child substitutes the "d" sound. Many teachers will attempt to "correct" the African American child's pronunciation. Imagine, if you will, the impact on these two children—the French-speaking child and the African American child—when they receive their very different responses from their teacher. In the first instance, the child is encouraged, and in the latter, there is clear discouragement.

Another example stems from the premise in U.S. society that "competition for competition's sake" is a value held dear by everyone. In fact, this is an alien value for many children who are not of European extraction.

Cultural differences are also reflected in learning styles. For example, African American children (and all African children) are active learners. It is not uncommon in effective African American classrooms to see what appears to be disorder, apparent chaos, and numerous loud conversations simultaneously going on (Lomotey & Brookins, 1988; Wilson, 1978). Yet *many* teachers, unaware of this cultural distinction, resist teaching children who behave in this culturally different way. And more importantly, even if they wished to teach children who have this distinctive learning style, more often than not, they do not have the necessary pedagogical skills.

Our society, in general, discourages understanding, appreciation, and respect for cultural differences, and schools mirror that reality. For *Brown v. Board of Education* to even begin to fulfill its promise, we must begin to prepare teachers to adequately understand, appreciate, and respect cultural differences.

The Role of African-Centered Pedagogy

Thus far, we have spoken of the need for cultural equity in U.S. classrooms and for a culturally equitable pedagogy for all school children, whether their backgrounds are European, African, Asian, or Hispanic. However, it seems clear that African American students also need an African-centered pedagogy as a fundamental part of their educational experience. Such a pedagogy is necessary for African American children to make sense of the life conditions that many of them experience and, more importantly, to enable them to resist the forces that imposed these conditions upon them (Lee et al., 1993). Such a pedagogy is also necessary to "produce an education that contributes to achieving pride, equity, power, wealth, and cultural continuity" for African Americans (Lee et al., 1993).

Perhaps most importantly, an African-centered pedagogy is necessary to nurture ethical character development that leads to ethical social practice in the African American community. Certainly, a critical component of an African American ethos is the restoration of the African American male as husband, father, provider, protector, and sustainer of the family.

Teachers, School Leaders, and the School Environment

For pedagogy to be transformed, school leaders and teachers must be transformed as well. This, of course, is a monumental task, and a task that federal courts overlooked while they were overseeing school district desegregation cases. Efforts were made to desegregate the teaching forces as well as the student bodies of segregated school districts; however, by and large, the courts made no effort to improve the quality of the teaching forces in the districts that went under court-ordered desegregation plans.

Various commentators have made useful suggestions for improving the quality of the teaching force and for increasing the number of African American teachers (Murnane et al., 1991). Better pay and working conditions for beginning teachers are critical, particularly in urban districts where large numbers of poor children and children with special needs make the jobs of beginning teachers especially challenging. More time for teachers to plan, reflect, and collaborate would also help (Natriello et al., 1990, pp. 167 – 170), along with better preservice and professional development training in the real-life challenges of urban schools.

On the issue of teacher quality, two problems deserve special mention. First, many inner-city teachers experience ''burnout'' long before they reach retirement age (Dworkin, 1987). Faced with the intractable problems of the inner-city schools, their energy, creativity, and commitment often fade several years before they leave classroom teaching. Second, as professional opportunities expand for the nation's best-educated African Americans, schools find it increasingly difficult to attract these people into teaching. In terms of remuneration and prestige, education simply cannot compete with law, medicine, or business.

Both of these problems can be addressed by developing better incentives for recruiting dedicated teachers for inner-city schools – not for a lifetime – but for shorter periods of time, perhaps three to seven years.

With proper incentives, idealistic and energetic individuals could be encouraged to become inner-city teachers for a few years and to leave before becoming burned out. Outstanding African Americans could devote a portion of their working life to teaching – either in mid-life, late in their careers, or prior to beginning postgraduate professional training.

Currently, teacher salary scales, teacher retirement systems, and state certification standards work together to penalize short-term teaching commitments. People who wish to teach for shorter periods of time must start at the bottom of the pay scale, with no recognition for experience in another vocation. In addition, depending on the state they live in, potential teaching recruits must complete a time-consuming series of college-level education courses before becoming certified. Finally, people who desire to spend a limited number of years teaching before pursuing another profession are faced with the prospect of losing their retirement contributions if they leave teaching before vesting in the teachers' retirement system.

What kinds of incentives would encourage high-quality, short-term teachers? First, streamlined alternative certification requirements – already implemented in some states – would reduce the opportunity costs for people who wish to become teachers either before or after pursuing other careers. Second, salary schedules could be constructed to reward new teachers for experience gained outside the education field. Finally, teachers' retirement systems should be designed like those in place for college faculty members so that teachers could claim 100 percent of their retirement contributions when they resign, whether or not they teach for one year or for thirty.

Obviously, we would not want all of the nation's teachers to be short-time educators. Nor would we want a school's entire teaching staff to be trained through a short-cut alternative certification process. Career teachers and instructional leaders – people who devote their entire working lives to education – should always form the core personnel of the public schools. Moreover, traditionally certified educators – people knowledgeable about curriculum, child development, and learning theory – will probably always be key to developing a sound learning environment. But public education should have a place – particularly in the inner-city schools – for committed individuals who want to dedicate a few years (early in a career, mid-career, or late in life) to public school teaching. Providing such places might attract some of the nation's most able African American college graduates into the teaching profession, and it might also reduce the number of burned out teachers who currently work in the nation's inner-city schools.

Ultimately, however, inner-city schools will not be successful because we hit upon exactly the right restructuring plan, the perfect reform strategy, or the correct school organization model. Schools will be successful when they are staffed by compassionate, energetic, and creative educators. Although U.S. schools have such educators by the thousands, too often, they are in short supply in the schools that African American children attend. This is why it is important for educators at all levels to reflect on their personal biographies, consider how they feel about the students whom they are charged with educating, and work in concert with them to alter the status quo—to change the power relationships that exist in schools and in U.S. society.

How will we know when our inner-city schools have adequate numbers of such educators? We will know when we see a transformed school environment. In particular, when the school environment is transformed, educators will not allow adversarial collective bargaining tactics to prevail over the interests of children. Schools will be clean and well-maintained, because the demands of the custodians unions will be subordinate to our children's need for a safe and attractive place to learn. Corporal punishment will be abolished, along with sloppy teacher recruiting practices, fraud, and mismanagement. Children will be protected from violence, and childhood sexual abuse by school employees will be punished, instead of covered up. In short, when inner-city school environments are transformed, African American children will find schools where they are welcomed, honored, nurtured, and kept safe.

CONCLUSION

We preface our concluding remarks by stating that we do not believe that U.S. public schools—as presently structured—can effectively educate African American children. Even if education is defined in its narrowest sense—merely obtaining a diploma—the high school dropout rates in urban African American communities attest to the fact that public education for African Americans has largely been a failure. If education is defined as nurture, life enrichment, cultural reinforcement, and fulfillment of potential, then the failure is even more stark.

To be sure, courts have played a crucial role in desegregating schools. But in the litigation process, we neglected the original concern: improving the achievement and life chances of African Americans. Although we were sometimes successful in getting white and African American children into the same school, we failed to prepare teachers who could effectively respond to children's cultural differences.

We can begin addressing this critical oversight by (a) introducing culturally equitable pedagogy in the classroom and by supporting African-centered pedagogy in districts with large numbers of African American students; (b) providing effective, competent, and compassionate teachers and school leaders to the children who need them most; (c) reorganizing our schools into safe and nurturing environments for children; and (d) honestly addressing issues of inequality in society and schools.

In other words, we must do more than desegregate our schools; we must transform them into places where African American children can be successful. We are not doing that now, and every day, African American children and society as a whole pay part of the price for our failure.

REFERENCES

Advocate staff (1995, April 9). Thin paddles ordered 1,000 at a time. *Sunday (Baton Rouge) Advocate,* p. 2B.

Beck, L. (1995, April 9). Principals: Many parents OK disciplinary paddling. *Sunday (Baton Rouge) Advocate,* p. 2B.

Bell, D. A. (1983). The final hurdle: Class-based roadblocks to racial remediation. Paper presented to the Mitchell Lecture Committee of the SUNY Buffalo Law School, Buffalo, NY.

Bennett, C. E. (1995). *The black population in the United States: March 1994 and 1993.* Washington, DC: U.S. Bureau of the Census.

Bissinger, H. G. (1990). *Friday night lights.* New York: Harper Perennial.

Bradley, A. (1994, April 27). F.B.I. agent fills new Chicago post to probe waste, fraud. *Education Week,* p. 3.

Burch, P. (1992). *The dropout problem in New Jersey's big urban schools: Educational inequality and governmental inaction.* New Brunswick, NJ: Rutgers, Bureau of Government Research.

Celis, W., III. (1995, March 22). Education consultant faces career challenge as Philadelphia school chief. *The New York Times,* p. B7.

Dempsey, V. and Noblit, G. W. (1993). Cultural ignorance and school desegregation: Reconstructing a silenced narrative. *Educational Policy* 7(3):318–339.

Dworkin, A. G. (1987). *Teacher burnout in the public schools.* Albany, NY: State University of New York Press.

Eaton, S. (1994, January/February). Forty years after *Brown,* cities and suburbs face a rising tide of racial isolation. *Harvard Education Letter,* p. 1.

Feldman, J., Kirby, E., and Eaton, S. E. (1994). *Still separate, still unequal: The limits of Milliken II's educational compensation remedies.* Cambridge, MA: Harvard Project on School Desegregation.

Flamm, S. R., Loughran, R. A., and Keith, L. (1992, November). *A system like no other: Fraud and misconduct by New York City custodians.* New York: New York City Office of the Special Commission of Investigation.

Fossey, R. (1993). Site-based management in a collective bargaining environment: Can we mix oil and water? *International Journal of Educational Reform* 2:320–324.

Fossey, R. and Garvin, J. (1995, February 22). Cooking the books on dropout rates, *Education Week,* p. 48.

Fossey, R. and Miles, K. (1992). School based management in the Boston Public Schools: Why isn't it working? Unpublished paper prepared for the Boston Mayor's Office.

Gartner, A. and Lipsky, D. K. (1989). *The yoke of special education: How to break it.* Rochester, NY: National Center on Education and the Economy.

Graham, P. A. (1993). What America has expected of its schools over the past century. *American Journal of Education* 101(2):83–98.

Hilliard, A. G. (1988). Conceptual confusion and the persistence of group oppression through education. *Equity and Excellence,* 24(1):36–43.

Hyman, I. A. (1990). *Reading, writing, and the hickory stick: The appalling story of physical and psychological abuse in American schools.* Lexington, MA: Lexington Books.

Jackson, F. (1993–1994). Seven ways to culturally responsive pedagogy. *Journal of Reading* 37:298–303.

Kennedy, E. (1993, July). *A study of out-of-school suspensions and expulsions in Louisiana schools.* Research Report 93-1. Baton Rouge, LA: Louisiana Department of Education.

Ladson-Billings, G. (1994). *The dream keeper: Successful teachers of African American children.* San Francisco: Jossey-Bass.

Lee, C. D., Lomotey, K., and Shujaa, M. (1993). How shall we sing our sacred song in a strange land. In H. S. Shapiro and D. E. Purpel (Eds.) *Critical social issues in American education* (pp. 179–193). New York: Longman.

Lomotey, K. (1989). Cultural diversity in the urban school: Implications for principals. *NASSP Bulletin,* pp. 81–85.

Lomotey, K. and Brookins, C. (1988). The independent black institutions: A cultural perspective. In D. T. Slaughter and D. J. Johnson (Eds.), *Visible now: blacks in private schools* (pp. 163-183). Westport, CT: Greenwood.

Marks, P. (1993, August 8). Asbestos tests were faked, officials say. *The New York Times,* p. 37.

Miles, K. H. (1993, June). *Rethinking school spending: A case study of Boston Public Schools.* Cambridge, MA: National Center for Educational Leadership.

Moore, D. and Davenport, S. (1990). School choice: The new improved sorting machine. In L. Boyd and J. J. Walberg (Eds.), *Choice in education: Potential and problems* (pp. 187–223). Berkeley, CA: McCutchan.

Murnane, R. J., Singer, J. D., Willett, J. B., Kemple, J. J., and Olsen, R. J. (1991). *Who will teach? Policies that matter.* Cambridge, MA: Harvard University Press.

National Center for Education Statistics (1991). *Characteristics of the 100 largest public elementary and secondary school districts in the United States: 1988–1989.* Washington, D.C.: U.S. Department of Education.

National Center for Education Statistics (1994). *Digest of education statistics 1994.* Washington, D.C.: U.S. Department of Education.

Natriello, G., McDill, E. L., and Pallas, A. M. (1990). *Schooling disadvantaged children: Racing against catastrophe.* New York: Teachers College Press.

Ogbu, J. (1986). The consequences of the American caste system. In U. Neisser (Ed.), *The school achievement of minority children.* Hillandale, NJ: L. Elbaum Associates.

Orfield, G. and Monfort, F. (1988). *Racial change and desegregation in large school districts: Trends through 1986–1987 school year.* Alexandria, VA: National School Boards Association.

Parham, W. and Parham, T. (1989). The community and academic achievement. In G. Berry and J. Asamen (Eds.), *Black students: Psychosocial issues and academic achievement* (pp. 120–137). Newbury Park, CA: Sage.

Report: D.C. schools employ hundreds with criminal records (1995, April 26). *Education Week,* p. 4.

Richardson, L. (1994, April 6). Minority students languish in special education system. *The New York Times,* p. A1.

Sack, K. (1993, November 17). Controls approved for custodians in New York City's public schools. *The New York Times,* p. A16.

Schmidt, P. (1993, September 29). Throwing light on dark corners of N.Y.C.'s bureaucracy. *Education Week,* p. 15.

Schmidt, P. (1995, May 3). Council moving to gain more say over D.C. schools. *Education Week,* p. 1.

Singletary, C. (1992). Academic effectiveness of elementary magnet schools. Unpublished doctoral dissertation. State University of New York at Buffalo, Buffalo, NY.

Stanfield, J. H. (1982). Urban public school desegregation: The reproduction of normative white domination. *Journal of Negro Education,* 51(2):90–100.

Stein, N. D. (1993, January). Sexual harassment in schools, administrators must break the casual approach to objectionable behavior. *Administrator,* pp. 14–19.

Tye, L. (1991, January 5). U. S. sounds retreat in school desegregation. *Boston Globe,* p. 1.

Willie, C. V. (1988). *Effective education: A minority policy perspective.* Westport, CT: Greenwood.

Wilson, A. N. (1978). *The developmental psychology of the Black child.* New York: African Research.

CHAPTER 12

Improving Our Children's Future: Looking Beyond Law-Based School Reforms

> *How small, of all that human hearts endure, that part which laws and kings can cure.*
>
> —Oliver Goldsmith, *The Traveller*

In the preceding chapters, we reviewed some of the many educational reform initiatives that have appeared over the past twenty years. Although some scholars have attempted to identify themes and trends in the school reform movement, the reality is that all these proposals are a hodgepodge of conflicting theories and political brokering, without much evidence of sustained commitment or vision.

Although these school reform initiatives reflect a wide variety of strategies and philosophies, they all had two things in common. First, each was a school reform effort based on law—whether it was a school reform bill passed by a state legislature, a court decision rendered by a state or federal judge, or a local mandate shaped through collective bargaining or a school board policy. Second, each school reform effort was driven by a fixed belief that something is wrong with the way the nation educates its children.

We preface our concluding chapter by saying clearly that we agree with this second fundamental conviction: something is indeed wrong with the way American children are educated. Not everywhere, of course. As Robert Reich (1991) and others have pointed out, the children of America's elite receive the finest education in the world. Children

183

who attend prestigious private schools, selective admission public schools like Boston's Latin School, or the well-funded and well-staffed schools in the nation's affluent suburbs have every educational advantage. These children receive foreign language instruction; they have access to computers; they are exposed to enriching travel, art, and music; and they are taught by instructors skilled in teaching critical thinking, problem solving, collaboration, and research. In these schools, we have little to worry about.

But in many of our schools, in particular, our inner-city schools and schools in impoverished rural areas, hundreds of thousands of children are ill-served. Drop-out rates are quite high in the inner cities, hovering around 50 percent in many urban districts. Among those who do graduate from these schools, many do not have basic reading skills on the day they receive their diplomas. The situation for many African American youth is desperate all across urban America; for these youth, their high school experience often provides them almost no assistance in obtaining a job or pursuing postsecondary education.

It has been the theme of this book that law-based school reform initiatives have had little effect on the nation's troubled urban school districts or on schools in the impoverished regions of rural America. In fact, for children living in these environments, conditions have often worsened.

Litigation – to single out one reform strategy – has utterly failed to fulfill its promise of improving educational opportunities. Two generations of children have gone to school since the Supreme Court ordered the Topeka schools desegregated in *Brown v. Board of Education,* yet African American students continue to be racially isolated in many cities, and in northern cities more than southern. More than thirty years have passed since the California Supreme Court, in *Serrano v. Priest,* declared that children going to school in poor communities should receive substantially equal financial resources as children living in wealthy towns. Yet the children of the poor are still not given the educational opportunities available to the children of the rich, even in the states where courts have followed the lead of the California Supreme Court and issued their own *Serrano*-type decisions.

Shared decision making and site-based management proposals, such as the much-heralded schemes introduced in Dade County, Florida, and Rochester, New York, have not altered schooling conditions in many of the schools where they were adopted. Five years after embracing shared

decision making, who would say that the educational experiences of Rochester children or Dade County children are fundamentally different from the experience of children living in Cleveland, Washington, D.C., or the Bronx?

As for the hundreds of educational reform laws passed by the states over the past twenty years, not one has altered the fundamental way children are educated. Indeed, it would be difficult to point to any single piece of legislation and proclaim that, because this particular law was passed by state A's legislature, the children of state A are qualitatively better off than the children of the other forty-nine states.

Why have two decades of school reform legislation, litigation, and law-based policy initiatives produced so little? We believe there are three fundamental explanations.

First, virtually all school reform activity during the past twenty years was carefully crafted to avoid tampering with the interests of powerful education interest groups—school boards and teachers' unions in particular. Charter school laws (to name one currently popular reform idea) have been passed in more than twenty states. But when these laws are examined in detail, it is evident that they were carefully crafted to avoid any major changes in the way most schools operate. As of this writing, only a handful of charter schools have actually begun operating, leaving the vast majority of the nation's 15,000 school districts unaffected. And in Massachusetts, an omnibus school reform act was passed in 1993 without addressing school consolidation, a need that was clearly identified by state educators more than fifty years ago. Thus, the state continues to have school districts with less than 200 students.

Of course, it is the teachers' unions that have been most successful in riding out the successive waves of school reform without having to make any significant adjustments to the way they do business. Indeed, to a large extent, they have managed to maintain the image that they are in the vanguard of change while opposing substantive reforms at every turn. We have seen teachers' associations fight—in legislative halls and in the courts—such reforms as charter schools, postsecondary school options, school choice, teacher testing proposals, and a host of other innovations.

Not only have the unions often opposed substantive reform proposals, they have clung tenaciously to an industrial model of labor relations, which is a serious barrier to improving school environments. As we said in earlier chapters, we do not believe any significant change in public

education will take place until an alternative is found to adversarial labor relations in the schools. Particularly in the inner-city districts – where education problems are most acute and where labor relations are often the most hostile – some alternative must be found to a system that defines teachers and administrators as enemies.

Second, while school reformers focused on such things as organizational change, legal developments, governance, and accountability, very little attention was paid to the quality of people presently working with children. To reiterate what we said in an earlier chapter, no reform initiative, no matter how brilliant and comprehensive, will be successful if the educators who implement it are incompetent or indifferent. To put it another way, it is difficult to see how shared decision making will transform a school environment where it is virtually impossible to remove a convicted drug dealer from the classroom.

Part of the quality problem stems from the fact that law-based reforms have been unable to hold educators accountable for their professional conduct. Other professionals – doctors and lawyers, for example – are held legally responsible for their negligence and can be sued for the injuries they cause. However, as Terri DeMitchell explained earlier in this book, the courts have unanimously rejected malpractice actions against educators. Although courts have sometimes held teachers to high standards of moral conduct outside the classroom, they have not provided a speedy avenue for removing substandard teachers who engage in school-related misbehavior.

Third, while we have espoused the easy platitude that ''all children can learn,'' thereby implying that all children *will* learn if the right reform theory is adopted, the real-life condition of many children has gotten worse (Annie E. Casey Foundation, 1994). Poverty, child neglect, and the erosion of intact, supportive families have reduced the effectiveness of all the nation's school reform efforts. To cite one stark statistic, almost one child in three is now born to an unmarried mother, and among African Americans, 68 percent of children are born to unmarried women (Blankenhorn, 1995, p. 301, n. 3). We are naive at best, and duplicitous at worse, to suggest that charter schools, family choice schemes, or school restructuring programs can successfully counteract this disastrous social trend.

We conclude now by saying that, in spite of our skepticism about the school reform efforts of the last two decades, we still believe that substantial improvements can be made in the way we nurture and educate

the nation's children. Nevertheless, if schools are to improve in fundamental ways, we must do more than merely tinker with the status quo. Our suggestions are not comprehensive, but we think they constitute a good start.

QUALITY OF TEACHERS AND EDUCATIONAL LEADERS

First, we need to pay more attention to the quality of the people who teach American school children. We do not believe the teaching force is mediocre as a whole; quite the contrary. The nation has thousands of dedicated and creative educators. But a significant number of school districts have serious problems with teacher quality, and the public's perception that it is virtually impossible to discharge an incompetent tenured teacher is largely correct.

What can we do to improve the quality of the teaching force? Much could be accomplished if school leaders simply did a better job of recruiting. As Richard Murnane and colleagues (1991) pointed out in their study of the nation's teaching force, there are enormous differences in the way school districts recruit teachers. These scholars concluded that one of the most important reasons to maintain teacher licensing requirements is to prevent some districts from doing an even worse job than they are already doing regarding the selection of teachers. In particular, many districts continue to make hiring decisions based on patronage considerations, rather than a teacher's skill level or dedication.

Unfortunately, although licensing requirements may prevent some districts from hiring teachers who are not even minimally qualified, they also discourage many talented college students from pursuing a teaching career. In many states, prospective teachers are required to take a large number of education courses in order to become licensed. As Murnane et al. (1991) pointed out:

> Extensive preservice training requirements deter many talented college students who would like to teach from ever doing so. Some never teach because they attend colleges that do not offer accredited teacher training programs, a lack that prevents students from pursuing a late-developing interest in teaching. Others, who do attend schools with approved programs, never teach because the required preservice courses appear dull and unrelated to the job of teaching and because completing the requirements reduces opportunities to take courses in other fields, includ-

ing the liberal arts and business. Students may be reluctant to forgo classes that would enhance their competitive position in applying for other jobs if they decide to leave teaching. (p. 89)

It is clear that burdensome licensing requirements are at least one of the factors that deter talented college graduates from entering the teaching field. Academically superior college graduates are less likely to enter teaching than less talented graduates, and private schools, which usually have no licensing requirements, hire teachers with higher standardized test scores than teachers who work in the public schools (Murnane et al., 1991).

We are not suggesting that certification requirements be eliminated altogether or that subject matter expertise is all that is required to produce an excellent teacher. Teachers need to master more than their discipline; they need to understand child development and learning theory as well. Nevertheless, we think the core knowledge base of the teaching profession can be imparted effectively in many different ways. Alternative licensing requirements, which would make it easier for noneducation majors to enter the teaching force, would almost certainly improve the pool of qualified teachers.

Not only do we need to make it easier for talented college graduates to teach, we also need to develop ways to attract outstanding individuals from business and industry into the teaching field, if only for a few years. As Lomotey and Fossey pointed out in an earlier chapter, teacher salary scales currently reward teachers based solely on years of service and educational attainment. An experienced businessperson, or even a college professor who wants to teach in the public schools for a few years, must start at the bottom of the salary scale, with no credit given for other work experience. In many states, short-term teaching commitments are discouraged by regulations that require teachers to forfeit part of their retirement contributions if they leave teaching before becoming vested in the state teacher retirement system—typically five years or more.

Revising licensing requirements, altering teacher retirement programs, and developing more flexible teacher salary scales are easy to do as a technical matter, but these innovations threaten a nationwide system of training and compensating teachers based on the notion that teaching is a guild with membership contingent on completing a standard teacher-education curriculum and compensation based largely upon length of service. Thus, improving the quality of the teaching force involves more than a few regulatory changes; it requires a new way of looking at teaching, one that is more flexible about teacher preparation and more accepting of fluidity between teaching and other occupations.

Of course, just as important as the quality of teachers is the quality of school administrators. As Kent D. Peterson and Chester E. Finn, Jr. (1985) observed in an insightful article, ''Practically never does one encounter a good school with a bad principal or a high-achieving school system with a low-performance superintendent.'' The authors pointed out that there are less than 100,000 principals and superintendents in the United States, and any policy changes that affect this relatively small number of educators could have an enormous impact on the overall quality of our schools.

Peterson and Finn make a number of useful suggestions for improving the quality of the nation's school administrators, suggestions with which we largely concur. Colleges and universities need to be a great deal more selective in accepting candidates to educational administration graduate programs, and these programs need to become more focused on leadership, problem solving, and practical research. Principals and superintendents need to be trained as instructional leaders — people knowledgeable about curriculum, child development, and learning theory — and not merely as bureaucratic managers and public relations artists.

We also believe that our expectations for school administrators need to be elevated. In many districts, particularly in communities that place a high value on high school athletics, school principals and superintendents are drawn almost exclusively from the coaching ranks. Too often, these ex-coaches have no broad vision about children's educational needs. In other districts, administrative positions are patronage jobs, which are dispensed by politically motivated school boards with no regard for a candidate's educational philosophy or moral leadership. And in some of our largest urban districts, school superintendents have become almost fungible commodities, flitting from city to city every few years (Casserly, 1995), often switching districts after running into political difficulties with local school board members. Superintendents' contracts are now being bought out by disaffected school boards with such frequency that the practice has almost become routine.

In our view, improving leadership at the top is not simply a matter of legislative reform. We need to do a number of things. First, we need to expand the pool of executive leadership to include more women, business leaders, and people from higher education. As we stated earlier regarding teachers, superintendent licensing requirements must be eased for this to occur. In addition, we should require our education executives to make long-term commitments to particular communities. Superintendents who introduce school reform initiatives with great fanfare should stick around long enough to ensure their success and to be accountable for reforms that falter. We also believe that executive leaders should play by the same rules that apply to classroom teachers, instead of taking on the trappings of corporate executives. In far too many large school districts, the superintendent is given a generous salary, enhanced retirement benefits, an expense account, and an extravagant travel allowance. Meanwhile, classroom teachers labor in dirty and often unsafe surroundings, without offices, adequate planning time, or even a place to make private telephone calls to parents. Just as we need to narrow the gap between corporate executives' salaries and assembly line workers' pay, we also need to make sure that the working conditions of executive educators and classroom teachers are more comparable.

Finally, to return to the theme of an earlier chapter, we must do a better job of removing incompetent, immoral, and lazy employees from the education community. And as we said previously, this is not simply a matter of legislative reform. School boards and administrators could do more to improve their schools by insisting on competent performance by educators than by implementing the entire range of legislative reform measures that have been introduced over the past two decades.

Improving teacher quality is not the sole responsibility of school boards and administrators. In fact, it has been a mistake to place most of the burden of removing substandard teaching employees on the backs of school principals. Teachers, too, have a strong interest in maintaining high standards for educators. Just as parents want creative and dedicated teachers for their children, teachers want to work with competent colleagues. We think teachers are willing to do more to improve the teaching ranks than they have so far been asked to do and that a strong role needs to be created for them to do so.

Ultimately, however, the responsibility for improving the teaching force extends beyond the education profession. We will not begin to purge the ranks of unsatisfactory school employees until everyone involved with public education—administrators, teachers' unions, school boards, judges, and state legislators—recognize that a school child's need for compassionate, energetic, and dedicated teachers is at least as important as the right of a public employee to receive a paycheck.

NEW LABOR RELATIONS MODELS

Second, to summarize a major premise of this book, we need to develop new labor relations models for the schools. These new models must foster collegiality among educators, not enmity. Almost everyone would agree with this proposition as a generality; the popularity of site-based management legislation and shared decision making schemes testifies to that. Nevertheless, when these initiatives are actually implemented, we see that they are often mere window dressing, a thin veneer of civility over an adversarial labor relations model almost identical to the one that prevails in coal mines and steel mills.

Not enough research and dialogue about labor relations in the schools has been conducted to sketch out a comprehensive reform proposal, but we think any worthwhile reform model will contain at least two important changes. First, disputes between teachers' groups and school boards would be resolved internally by the educators directly responsible for the welfare of children and not delegated through grievance processes to arbitrators, who are usually labor lawyers, to decide.

Second, the responsibility for defending teachers charged with immorality, incompetence, or insubordination should be placed on some independent agency—not the teachers' unions. The current practice of having teachers' association representatives assume the burden of defending these teachers has encouraged them to develop a hostile attitude towards school authorities and has made them virtually indistinguishable from the business representatives for the Teamsters and Steel Workers unions. School union leaders need to shift from their adversarial role to becoming dispute resolution facilitators, curriculum specialists, and experts in marshaling community resources for children and families.

Thus far, the leading writers of the current school reform movement have shirked from a critical examination of teachers' unions and collective bargaining. With very few exceptions, one will search in vain in the school reform literature for even the appearance of the word *union*. Perhaps scholars and commentators fear being labeled anti-labor if they venture to criticize the industrial model of labor relations in our schools. What is needed, we believe, is a new atmosphere for discussing working conditions and co-worker relations in the schools—one that abandons the strife-laden rhetoric of traditional labor relations and begins with the fundamental understanding that all people who work in schools are colleagues, not adversaries, with much more in common than in dispute.

Are the unions ready to explore new labor relations models? We think they are. Several union leaders have acknowledged the need for fundamental change in the way educators work together. For example, Mary Hatwood Futtrell (1989), former president of NEA, has observed, "Teachers cannot hope to prepare students for the Information Age if they themselves are condemned to organizational structures derived from the Industrial Age." And Adam Urbansky (In Rochester, 1987), vice president of AFT, has expressed concern about a teaching profession in which teachers are both powerless and unaccountable.

One thing seems certain. Inflammatory attacks on the teachers' unions will not foster a better model of labor relations for the schools. If the teachers' unions too often adopt the posture of Depression-era industrial unions, their critics too frequently employ the rhetoric of Depression-era corporate bosses. Collegiality in the schools will not emerge until all the parties to traditional collective bargaining recognize and respect the core interests of the others.

A BROADER COMMITMENT TO IMPROVING THE CONDITION OF CHILDREN

Finally, school reform will not be successful unless the overall welfare of children improves. Unfortunately, while the education community focused on standardized tests, accountability provisions, school choice models, and curriculum innovations, the condition of American children worsened. This trend cannot be reversed solely by changing what goes on within the four walls of a classroom.

The education community has not been indifferent to social and political issues affecting children, nor has it closed its eyes to the environments in which children live. Schools have begun linking with community agencies to provide better health and social services, and some have been active in drug education, AIDS awareness, and various kinds of violence prevention efforts. Nevertheless, we can do more in this area.

For example, most educators' professional groups are on record as opposing corporal punishment in the schools. Yet more than twenty states still permit educators to inflict physical pain on children. If education interest groups had worked as actively for the abolition of corporal punishment as they have for increased funding and better employment benefits, corporal punishment would now be a thing of the past.

Likewise, most educators' groups have been silent about the growth of state-sponsored gambling, which has been promoted in many states as a way to generate more education revenues. It is now clear that legalized gambling has led to increased crime and government corruption in some states, that it disproportionately attracts the poor, and that it has not provided additional money for public education (Jones & Amalfitano, 1994; Garland, 1995). Educators, through their professional groups, could make a significant effort toward improving children's environments if they actively opposed the spread of government-sponsored gambling in their states.

Gun control is another area where educators' voices should be louder and more strident. Educators have been embroiled in a high-profile debate about AIDS education in schools, which is an important issue, to be sure. But there are far more pediatric deaths from firearms than from AIDS. As Donna Shalala, U.S. Secretary of Health and Human Services, aptly observed, gun violence is not just a criminal problem; it is a public health epidemic (California Wellness Foundation, 1995). Public educators, through their professional organizations, would advance children's health and safety measurably if they began vigorously promoting gun control.

We are not arguing for political activism as a substitute for law-based school reform initiatives. Indeed, the child welfare issues that we just identified will all require new legislation in order to better protect children's interests. We believe, however, that the education community's focus on school reform has often been too narrow, with too little attention paid to the larger social forces that threaten children's well-being. Unless we intervene, and intervene more effectively, in these social issues, we cannot hope to improve educational outcomes for children to the extent that is necessary.

When all is said and done, nurturing children and preparing them for a place in the adult world cannot be accomplished through a legal formula or decreed by judicial order. By pretending otherwise, educators—administrators, policymakers, professional organizations, teachers, researchers, and scholars—deceive themselves. And by doing so while the condition of children deteriorates, they put children and our society in jeopardy.

Educating children is a time-consuming and labor-intensive process, requiring creativity, dedication, sacrifice, and love. We can best achieve our aims, not by passing laws and filing lawsuits, but by maintaining high standards for the people who work in our schools, by putting the interests of children above that of adult interest groups, and by becoming more involved in efforts to improve the overall welfare of children in our society. Unless we do these things, let's not pretend that we are serious about educational reform.

REFERENCES

Annie E. Casey Foundation. (1994). *Kids count data book: State profiles of child well-being.* Greenwich, CT: Author.

Blankenhorn, D. (1995). *Fatherless America: Confronting our most urgent social problem.* New York: Basic Books.

California Wellness Foundation (1995). *The campaign to prevent handgun violence against kids: A report on the February 22, 1995 statewide videoconference.* San Rafael, CA: Author.

Casserly, M. (1995, August 14). Too much despair in the search for a chancellor. *New York Times,* p. A11.

DeMitchell, T. A. (1995). Competence, documentation, and dismissal: A legal template. *International Journal of Educational Reform* 4(10):88−95.

Futtrell, M. H. (1989). Mission not accomplished: Education reform in retrospect. *Phi Delta Kappan* 71:8−15.

Garland, G. (1995, July 30). Crime rising with gambling. *Sunday (Baton Rouge) Advocate,* p. 1.

In Rochester: Contract with teachers puts the interests of students first. (1987, November 5). *Philadelphia Inquirer,* p. A01 (Local).

Jones, T. H. and Amalfitano, J. L. (1994). *America's gamble: Public school finance and state lotteries.* Lancaster, PA: Technomic.

Murnane, R. J., Singer, J. D., Willett, J. B., Kemple, J. J., and Olsen, R. J. (1991). *Who will teach? Policies that matter.* Cambridge, MA: Harvard University Press.

Peterson, K. D. and Finn, C. E. (1985). Principals, superintendents, and the administrator's art. *Public Interest,* 79:42−62.

Reich, R. (1991). *The work of nations: Preparing ourselves for 21st century capitalism.* New York: Knopf.

Todd A. DeMitchell has served as an elementary school teacher, assistant principal, principal, director of personnel and labor relations, and superintendent in the public schools of California. Currently, he is an associate professor in the administration and supervision program and the associate chair of the department of education at the University of New Hampshire. He has published over forty articles on school law, collective bargaining, and policy analysis. His book, *Teachers Unions and TQE: Building Quality Labor Relations* (with William Streshly) was published by Corwin Press. In addition, Professor DeMitchell writes a quarterly research column entitled the Legal Department for the *International Journal of Educational Reform*. He has been named to *Who's Who in Education, Who's Who in the West,* and *Who's Who in the East.* He received his bachelor's and a master's degree in history from the University of LaVerne. He also holds a master's degree from the University of California, Davis, a doctorate in education from the University of Southern California, and he was postdoctoral visiting scholar at Harvard University.

Richard Fossey is an associate professor of education law and policy and coordinator of the Higher Education Administration Program in the College of Education at Louisiana State University in Baton Rouge. He received his doctorate in education policy from Harvard University in 1993 and his law degree from the University of Texas School of Law in 1980. Prior to beginning an academic career, he practiced education law in Alaska, where he represented school boards in Aleut, Athabaskan, and Inuit communities. His research interests include education law, school choice, child abuse and neglect, and school reform. He is coauthor, along with Michael Clay Smith, of *Crime on Campus: Liability Issues and Campus Administration,* published by Oryx Press and the American Council on Education.

CONTRIBUTING AUTHORS

Mark Bateman is an assistant professor in the College of Education at Louisiana State University in Baton Rouge, where he teaches in the area of higher education administration. Professor Bateman received his Ed.D. degree from the University of Indiana. He is coeditor, along with Richard Fossey, of *Borrowing against the Future: Student Loans, Higher Education and Public Policy,* to be published by Teachers College Press. His research includes college choice and education policy.

Louann A. Bierlein is currently the Education Policy Advisor to Louisiana Governor Mike Foster. She was formerly director of the Louisiana Education Policy Research Center at Louisiana State University, and Assistant Director of Education and Social Policy Studies at the Morrison Institute for Public Policy, Arizona State University. She is a nationally recognized expert on education reform, especially in the area of charter schools and has published extensively on this topic. She is also the author of *Controversial Issues in Educational Policy,* published by Sage Publications, Inc.

Terri A. DeMitchell has been an elementary school teacher, an instructor at the University of New Hampshire, and an attorney where she practiced school law. She has published articles on library censorship and teacher out-of-school behavior. She received her bachelor's degree from San Diego State University (with honors), a master's degree in curriculum and instruction from the University of California, Davis, and her law degree from the University of San Diego School of Law. Currently, she is completing a graduate degree at Harvard University where she has studied literacy and policy. Terri has appeared in *Who's Who In Education, Who's Who in American Law,* and *Who's Who of American Women.*

Kofi Lomotey is chair and professor in the Department of Administrative and Foundational Services in the College of Education at Louisiana State University in Baton Rouge. His research interests include African American principals, independent African-centered schools, issues of race in higher education, and urban education. Professor Lomotey is the editor of the journal *Urban Education.* In addition, he serves on the editorial boards of several journals, including *Educational Administration Quarterly* and *Journal for a Just and Caring Education.*